MW01268106

Also by CaSaundra W. Foreman:

The Motherless Children

When An Angel Takes Flight/The Light

Thank you
for mentoring me!
Love, Peace
Prosperity, Miracles
& Blessings
To You!
CaSaundra Foreman

THE DETERMINATION OF I

authorHOUSE®

AuthorHouse™
1663 Liberty Drive
Bloomington, IN 47403
www.authorhouse.com
Phone: 1-800-839-8640

First published by AuthorHouse 4/26/2011

ISBN: 978-1-4567-3284-4 (e)
ISBN: 978-1-4567-3285-1 (dj)
ISBN: 978-1-4567-3286-8 (sc)

Library of Congress Control Number: 2011901051

Printed in the United States of America

-Dedicated to the memory of-

My mother, Lorene Halstied Foreman, (March 2, 1937-November 1, 2003)who was my first fan, and biggest supporter, but isn't here this time to get the first copy of my newest book.

Thank you for believing in me, encouraging me to always have a plan, and teaching me to be determined to do my best at whatever I set out to do.

For,
Marquis, LaBraska, Javonte & Mya

God grant me the serenity
to accept the things I cannot change,
the courage to change the things I can,
and the wisdom to know the difference.
- The Serenity Prayer

I can do all things through Christ, which strengthens me.
-Phil. 4:13

FOREWORD

Determination is defined as "unwavering firmness of character or action." There is no doubt that one must be determined to achieve success and accomplish goals in his/her life but this word has a more profound definition in my personal opinion. As a woman of faith, I believe that one's goals, aspirations and dreams must be built on the foundation of faith, belief and trust in God. Matthew 6:33 reads: "Seek ye first the kingdom of God and His righteousness and all these things will be added unto thee." As believers in Christ Jesus we know that nothing is impossible for God.

Over the years I have watched CaSaundra as she has faced the challenges of life with dignity, honor and character. She is strong in her faith in God, a loving and devoted mother and a positive role model.

I believe that as we travel on this journey we must be determined to love as God requires, to deny self, pick up the cross and follow Jesus. With this conviction, it is guaranteed that we will achieve success and accomplish goals according to God's divine plan and purpose for our lives and according to His will. Jeremiah 29:11 reads: "I know the thoughts that I think toward you, saith the Lord, thoughts of peace, and not of evil, to give you an expected end."

God Bless you, CaSaundra. Thank you for allowing God to stir up the gifts within so that you will not only be blessed but you will continue to be a blessing to others.
    Love, Mrs. Myrtle Clay Johnson

PREFACE

Everyone has a story. Everyone has a struggle, or an issue. Everyone has a choice to make; either persevere or give up. The stories shared in this book are of people who had the determination to make something happen. Each story is based on a true story, and a look into the personal issues real people face everyday.

People everywhere hope God gives them the strength they need to make it through each day. They pray for God to give them peace, and fix their problems. Some pray and wait patiently. Others, pray and pray some more. While some pray, and give up.

When the individual, the "I", has the will, the gumption, the heart, the courage, the soul, the belief, the mindset, the love, the determination to do something, things happen.

I pray you are encouraged to find the determination within yourself to make something positive happen in your life. If you can't find the determination inside you, ask God to give you the faith, strength and courage you need to defeat, overcome, empower, encourage, fight, win, pray, fulfill and laugh your way through life's ups and downs.

If you happen to find your story amongst these pages, realize you had something amazing and worthy of sharing. Continue to let your light shine before others, and God will continue to work a mighty work in your life.

To my friends, thanks for growing with me throughout life's stumbling blocks, joys and tearful moments. Thanks for sharing with me in life's triumphs, dramatic times and comical moments. Thanks for praying for me and with me, as I prayed for you, and thanks for making me a better person each day that I live. As we go through life, we are lucky if we meet one *good* friend. I am blessed to say God has given me more than my fair share.

~ CaSaundra W. Foreman

CONTENTS

GOING HOME

I am a mother, a grandmother, a sister, an aunt and a friend. I have always been an independent woman who worked hard to get ahead, and didn't mind working extra jobs to take care of my daughter, and my bills.

I was married twice, to the same man. We met after I graduated from high school. I loved him…more than I knew was possible. Even though, he cheated on me through the duration of our marriage.

Sometimes, it became too much to bare.

After finally deciding that my marriage wasn't going to work, I found myself going through a depression stage. I slept most of the time, and went to work, and came home. My daughter, who was a teenager at the time, was old enough to understand, and encouraged me that things would be just fine.

And, eventually they were. I stopped being sad, and was determined to live happily ever after.

Through the years, I found happiness in my single life, and was especially happy with my grandchildren. I have to admit, I spoiled them. That's a grandmother's job.

Some of the things I enjoyed indulging in the most were coffee, I could drink it morning, noon and night, Pepsi, Buttered Pecan Ice Cream and Pay Day candy bars. I loved to cook, baking especially. And Christmas was my favorite holiday. I loved decorating the tree, the house, buying Christmas presents, wrapping them with pretty paper and putting a bow on them for a personal touch. I loved to read, and I enjoyed watching Lifetime movies. My favorite Soap was *Days of Our Lives*, and I enjoyed watching *Gun Smoke* on Saturdays. Oh, yes, and that game show *Wheel of*

Fortune…I was real good at that! I found relaxation in sewing, and playing Scrabble. I was good at Spades and Bid Whist too.

I also enjoyed smoking cigarettes. It was a habit I had picked up while dating my ex-husband. I have to admit, when I met him, I was a square, as they called it in my day. I didn't drink alcohol, or smoke. When we went out with his friends, I chose to drink soda. My then boyfriend, and future ex-husband would tell me that I was going to have to choose something to be social. Either smoke cigarettes, or drink. Well, I didn't like the taste of alcohol. And, if I had known then that quitting smoking would be so hard, I would have chosen the alcohol. I could have just pretended to sip on a glass of watered down alcohol, and wouldn't have had a habit that was hard to get rid of. We live and learn.

Eventually, my years of smoking cigarettes caught up with me. I had tried to quit many times. I used the gum, the patch, tried some prescription pills, even quit cold turkey once. One day, after a visit to my doctor for a check up of my diabetes, I received a phone call from my doctor. She had bad news. I had cancer. Ironically, after receiving her news, I no longer had the desire for cigarettes.

I was devastated. I was crushed. I was angry. I became depressed. I began to sleep a lot. I…hid the news from my family. I even ignored the calls from my doctor's office.

My daughter began to notice that something was wrong. She started nosing around, and even spoke to my doctor. And even though my doctor wouldn't tell her exactly what was wrong with me, she told her enough to let her know it was serious.

I wish she hadn't. I was determined to die. Quietly. I didn't want people knowing my business. Hey, it was my decision…my choice to smoke all those years. So, I figured this was God's way of punishing me.

My daughter had always had this way of taking care of me, without me feeling taken care of. She didn't make me feel helpless, yet began to do things that she knew I needed her to do. I was the mama. She was the child. Yet, she switched roles with me in a way that allowed me to let my guard down. Yet still, I was determined to not be a burden to anyone. And, because of my determination to be head strong and independent, I slowly began to die inside.

Weeks after my daughter found out my condition, she began to take me to doctor's appointments. She asked so many questions. I know, she was concerned and wanted the best for me. I was impatient and could be uncooperative at times. As I smile to myself, I know I was difficult to get along with, but that was my nature.

At some point, I remember my daughter sitting next to me one day as I sat in my bedroom, feeling tired and ready to give up life. She looked at me and said, "Mother, I don't know what you want me to do, but whatever it is, I will get it done. You have cancer, and your doctor said there are different treatments available…"

I looked at her, and without hesitation, said, "I don't want chemo. I hear it makes you sick, and makes your hair fall out." I always did love my hair. I felt that if my hair wasn't right, even if my outfit was perfect, then I wasn't looking good.

I remember my daughter sighing, and looking at me with sad eyes, and forcing a smile. "Yes ma'am. Whatever you say. I just wanted to know what to do."

I squeezed her hand and told her that I knew she would do the right thing on my behalf. She was my angel, and had always been a loving and caring daughter.

I remembered how she sat at the hospital with her dad for days while he was dying. She didn't want to leave him. She felt like it was her job, as his child, to be by his bedside, just in case he woke up. As the days kept passing by, and the decision had been made to take him off the machines that were allowing him to live, she still felt the need to be with him… she said she didn't want him to die alone. She was there…even as he took his last breath. She described it as air being sucked out of her…just as he breathed one last time. She said it felt as if her heart would stop with his.

That wasn't the only time she'd sat with someone so they wouldn't have to die alone. She did the same hard and somber task for a close friend of mine who suffered a brain aneurism. I remember getting that phone call. My friend had been rushed to the hospital, and I was on her emergency call list. I called my daughter, and she immediately left work, and picked me up from home. She was in a frantic rush to get to the hospital. Once we arrived, she began asking the nurses and the doctor's questions. Being at the hospital made me nervous. I was mentally drained after being there for hours, but my daughter said we needed to stay so my friend wouldn't be by herself. After awhile, my friend's brother and sister-in-law arrived, so my daughter and I left. Sadly before leaving the hospital, we found out from the doctor that they didn't expect my friend to make it through the night. My daughter asked the nurse to call her if there were any changes in her condition throughout the night. The nurse, seeing how concerned my daughter was, promised to call. And she did.

About one o'clock in the morning. The nurse called to say that my friend's vitals had changed and that if we wanted to see her before she died, we would need to come immediately. My daughter called to tell me what the nurse had said. I didn't want to go to the hospital…but my daughter said she would go. She said she didn't want her to be by herself. As she rushed to the hospital, she later shared with me how she prayed for my friend, talked to her, and sang to her. The nurse came in and told my daughter that my friend was aware that she was there because her heart rate had increased. Other family members began to arrive…but none said anything. They just stood around…waiting. My daughter said she was glad that she had gotten there first to have time to share a few last moments that possibly helped my friend as she took her walk through the valley of the shadow of death.

As weeks went by, and my daughter began to share with our family and closest friends that I was ill, I began to feel my illness taking complete control of my body. I could tell my family thought I was going to die, because they started visiting more and more. It became too much at times. I just needed peace, and quiet. Sometimes, I just wanted to sleep. I didn't want to eat, or drink. Just sleep.

Friends would visit. People I hadn't seen in a while would stop by. One good friend, who was ill herself, would come and just sit with me for hours. We would watch TV. I slept most of the time. I guess she didn't care. She kept coming back. So I wouldn't be alone while my daughter was at work.

My sister came to stay. She was sick too. But she said she had to come see about me. We laughed some. Talked about different things. It had been awhile since we'd spent time together. It was nice.

One day some neighbors came by. They claimed they were coming to help. I was getting ready to take a bath, and one of them asked if I needed any help. I looked at my daughter, who was getting ready to go to work, and told her that when the day came that I couldn't bathe myself, then it was time for me to die. I told her I didn't want to be a burden to anyone. She looked at me and told me not to say that. She told me she would take care of me. I knew she would…but I knew I didn't want her to have to.

My time was winding down. I was coughing up blood.

The ambulance came to get me. They thought I was going to die.

My daughter was there, at the hospital. Watching over me. I remember her coming into the room after I had been there for a few days. She looked so sad, and tired. I knew she had been worrying. But she would never let me see her cry. She touched my hand, and I asked her why did she look so sad. Holding back her tears, she mustered a fake grin and softly said, "I'm not." She was never very good at lying. I could always tell when she wasn't telling the truth.

I heard whispering. I awoke to find my brothers and sisters sitting in my room. That night had been a bad one. The doctors thought I wouldn't make it through the night. But it wasn't my time. Somebody, a lot of somebody's, had been praying for me.

The room was freezing. My daughter was wrapped in a blanket. I knew she was uncomfortable. But she tried to make the best of it. For me. My temperature kept spiking. So the nurses had this idea of making my room cold. It worked. Shoot. They were really delaying my time with God.

I heard whispering outside my room. They thought I was asleep. The doctor was saying something about chemo. My daughter was saying I didn't want it. Good girl!

The nurses began bringing in new medicines. What were they doing? A few days went by. I started feeling…different. But, I was still determined that my time had come to die.

I heard voices outside my room again. The doctor. I didn't like him very much. I heard my brother's voice. Then my daughter's voice. The doctor's voice again. "We tried a dose of chemo. It should have had a positive affect. But ultimately, it's up to the will of the patient. I don't know why she isn't feeling better. I think she has given up." Smart doctor.

I was ready to GO!!! Didn't anyone understand?

My daughter lived in the hospital room with me for weeks. Family and friends would visit.

One day, I had a talk with God. I didn't open my eyes. I wouldn't eat. They thought I was asleep. But, I wasn't. Just talking things over with God. I heard my baby singing the Lord's Prayer. It sounded pretty. I heard her praying aloud. She was so strong. So brave. She was tired too. I could hear it in her voice. Yet, she was keeping her promise to take care of me. Tears rolled down my eyes. I felt her wipe my face.

I recalled my childhood. The lessons I learned growing up. I remembered going to every church service when I was a kid. My daddy was a deacon and my mother a deaconess, so whenever the doors of the church were open, we were there.

I remembered the trouble I got into with my younger brother. The times I thought I was going to die from being such a tomboy, and doing adventurous and dangerous things with my younger brother. I remember my brother showing me where Mother hid the Christmas presents. It was his way of proving to me that Santa wasn't real. I remembered riding down the top of a hill on the back of a bike with him, I almost died. But I didn't have sense to know that it wasn't safe. My brother was doing it, so I was to.

I remembered sneaking my little sister's white socks out of the drawer. She was so particular and thrifty. She always kept everything neat and clean. And, jawbreakers, penny jawbreakers. Daddy would give us a nickel a week and we would go to the store and buy stuff. My sister would buy a penny jawbreaker, and it would last her a week. The rest of us, our stuff would be gone the same day. Oh, I could think back to a lot of times when I thought I wasn't going to make it past my teenage years. I remembered the time I got into a fight, and the girl picked up a broken beer bottle and hit me in my face. I remembered the blood. It infuriated me, and made me even more determined to win that fight. And I did. But I was also left with an ugly scar above my eye. Those were the days. I didn't back down from anyone who messed with me. Then there were the times I got in trouble with my mother…like the time I snuck off and was gone all day when the company came to visit that normally stayed all day. If only I had known that that visit would be short. I got a whipping that day. And my mother didn't play when it came to whippings. I thought about Daddy, and how he hated to whip us. His whippings didn't even hurt. Smile. I thought back to my older brother burning up the strap my mother used to spank us with. She never did find out what happened to that strap. I thought about how my younger brother wished we had a bus so that he could sit next to the window, because only the older kids could sit next to the window in the car. Smile. Hmmm…my first dance, when my oldest brother gave me money so I wouldn't have to have some boy buy me anything, because then, as he put it, that boy would think I owed him something. Basketball…I was a great ball player. Oh, and there was the time I jumped out of the car with that boy who was supposed to give me a ride home, yet kept driving the wrong way. Hmmm. I knew I had two choices that day. If he didn't kill me, my mother would when she found out I was in his car. I was all scarred up, but I hid my scars from my mother, because I didn't want to have to explain to her how I had gotten them.

I thought about my jobs. My coworkers. My friends. My happy times. My sad times. My daughter. Becoming a grandmother. My trip to Vegas, and Chicago. Ooh, I had a good time.

On the second day of my quiet time with God, I heard my daughter's voice. "Mother, if you eat for me, even just a little, I promise to take you home."

I smiled to myself. When the next meal came, I ate, but I didn't open my eyes. A friend was there. Feeding me, and talking to me. Reminding me of the good times we had shared. Especially when we went shopping. She loved to shop…I loved to shop for sales! Those were some good times. Smile.

I heard voices in my room. Whispering. Some lady asking my daughter about a home health aide. I heard my daughter tell the lady no thanks. She said I was her mother, and she would take care of me.

She was good! The very next day, I heard her voice again. "Wake up mother! You're going home!" She said.

I opened my eyes. "Who said?" I wanted to know.

"I told you if you ate I would take you home," she said with a big grin on her face. She was gathering her things. Nurses were coming in and out. My room was very busy.

Within hours, I was in the back of an ambulance, smiling. I was headed home, to my house. I was so happy to see my house. The one I had worked hard to pay off early, no matter how many odd jobs I had to take to do it.

My daughter and a lot of my family were waiting for me inside. I was just glad to be home.

In my dreams, I saw my parents. Talked to them. They were both in heaven. I saw friends that were in heaven too.

As I lay in my bed, looking out the window, an angel came and sat beside my bed. As I reached up to run my fingers through my hair, I felt places that had no hair. I was saddened. I knew my daughter had done what she felt would help. But, I had been determined to go HOME, to heaven. I retreated into my sanctuary with God one more time. I heard music. My daughter was playing my favorite songs. It set the atmosphere. My time was winding up. I looked at the angel beside my bed. Tears rolled down my face. I asked God to take me home. He said, "Soon."

The next day, I heard my daughter tell my grandson that he needed to come talk to me. I was glad because I had some things I needed to tell him.

I was so glad to see him. He was sad, and afraid, and I knew it. He sat down in the chair next to my bed. I grabbed his hand. And we talked. He cried. So did I. I told him to be good, and make me proud. I told him to do his best in school and make memories. I encouraged him to do positive things with his life. I told him I would be watching over him…I'd be with him everyday, in spirit. I told him I loved him. He didn't say much. Mostly "yes ma'am," and "I love you, too".

My good friend came to visit the next day. She had flown in from out of state. Wow. She almost missed me. I was glad God had made me wait. She pulled up a chair next to my bed. She'd brought me a gift. It was an angel. A beautiful caramel-skin colored angel, who played music. It was beautiful. My daughter loved it. She would enjoy it for me, and care for it in my absence. How befitting. An angel, for my angel.

My friend talked to me. I didn't talk back with my voice. I tried to communicate with my eyes. My vocal chords were silent. And, even though I wished I could tell her how much it meant to me that she had come so far to see me, I knew my eyes were saying what my mouth couldn't. I cried. So did she.

That night, while the house was quiet, and there was no one there but my daughter, watching over me, and caressing me, God said, "ok."

I heard the doorbell. I heard voices. It was my brothers. They had come to sit with my baby. To keep watch over me, as they had done when we were children. I heard my daughter telling them that it was almost over. She sounded so sad. They went to sleep. My daughter didn't.

All night, she sat there, watching me. Touching me. I was thankful she was there. Glad I wasn't alone.

The early morning came. My daughter sang to me…"His eye is on the sparrow…" And He was watching over me.

I heard voices. My brothers. My good friend. The nurse who had come to help in my last moments. They were sad. Talking to my daughter. It was time. My breathing began to slow down. My daughter! I cried out to God. "Wrap your arms around her, please! I know this is hard for her. Help her Lord!"

I heard her voice. I heard her gasp! I heard her cry out. "Mama, I love you. Please mama. Don't go! I DID THE BEST I COULD TO TAKE

CARE OF YOU! I KNOW YOU WERE READY TO GO! BUT I'M NOT READY!"

Oh, God, help her! He assured me she would be alright. For I had raised her to be strong, and because she knew God, she would be okay. He promised to wipe away her tears, and that in due season, the pain would go away. I trusted Him.

I could still hear her crying. Could feel her touch. Could see her beautiful face. "Thank you Lord for watching over her, and for not letting her be here alone." I heard my brothers praying for me. I heard my friend crying.

And then, my determination had run it's course...God answered my prayers, and took me...home, to my mansion in the sky.

I left them loving memories and words of wisdom to think of each day. I am still watching over them.

"I'm going up yonder...I'm going up yonder. I'm going up yonder... to be with my Lord..."

That's the determination of I!

"Step by step, on the stairway to heaven
Goin' step, by step...

THE HARD WAY

My heart sank when I got the call.

I remember, I was driving from work. It had been a long day. Too much work. Not enough time. Glad the work day was over, food was on my mind. Then, the cell phone rang. It was a familiar tone. My son's.

"Mama, I've been arrested…" the voice on the other end said.

I became determined not to let this situation break my heart.

My heart pounded as I drove up to the jail. Getting out of my car, I was unsure of what to say to him, unsure of what to expect once I got inside the jail. I never thought…no mother ever wants to think that their child…their baby…would be in jail. I didn't raise him with morals and values to be here. So, I reminded myself, it's not my fault.

The guard at the gate was very nice. I have to admit, I was embarrassed to be there. As he gave me instructions as to where to go, I took a deep breath, and walked the long walk to where he was.

I was saddened to be there…yet glad he was alive. He wasn't a bad person. Had just chosen to make bad choices. Those choices had gotten him here…in a grey building, surrounded by wires and fences, with no freedom.

As I sat behind the glass window, I smiled as I saw him. He looked thin. He smiled at me. I held back my tears.

We made small talk. Twenty minutes went by fast. Our time was up.

One evening, as his situation crossed my mind, I sat down to write him a letter. I thought about what to say. Then changed my mind, knowing that I didn't want to make him feel like I was fussing at him. Knowing him as I did, I knew that he was sad and rethinking the wrong choices he had made.

Several days later, my phone rang. It was him. Calling collect. "Mama, I have had time to think about my choices. When I get out of here, I don't ever plan to come back. This isn't where I want to spend my life. I promise, I am going to make you proud of me some day."

I hung up the phone. Tears in my eyes. I thought back to the day he was born, and how he seemed to be smiling the first time I saw him. Older people called it gas…but I silently disagreed.

I remembered when he was two months old, and I walked into the room to find him lying in his basinet, his foot dangling over the top. Amazed, I looked in the basinet, to find him smiling up at me.

Like most mothers, I was determined to be a good mother, one who kept her child safe, made him feel loved, made him feel special, taught him right from wrong, taught him manners, "please and thank you"-the magic words. I read to him every day and provided him with what I thought he needed to succeed in life.

I remembered when he first talked at nine months, and walked at eleven months. I remembered holding him at night for hours on end because his stomach hurt. He was allergic to milk. Yet the doctors hadn't figured it out. Yet every time he drank it, the milk would curdle on his stomach, and he would vomit it back up. The doctor would say he had a virus, but I knew a virus didn't last that long. So, I stopped giving him milk. I remembered his first day at preschool, and then his preschool graduation picture. He was so cute with his cap and gown on. Smiling big, holding that graduation diploma in his hand, he was so proud. He had so many plans and dreamed of being a fireman/teacher/singer/movie star.

As he grew older, he maintained his grades and was a good student in school. And of course, he participated in athletics. At one point, he dreamed of going to the NBA. Little boys always have big dreams. Children. So cute, so funny, so full of energy and promise.

I didn't post my son's bail, so he had to stay in jail.

A few days before Mother's Day, I received a card in the mail from my son. I knew it was a Mother's Day card, so I decided to wait until Mother's Day to open it.

As the days went by slowly, I found myself feeling ill. Admitted into the hospital, it was determined that my blood pressure was high enough for me to have a stroke or a heart attack. After being monitored for a few days and placed on medication, my worst nightmare, I was able to go home.

As I sat on my bed, the Mother's Day card caught my eye. I wondered what it said. Wondered what it looked like. After all, my son hadn't been the most giving person in the world. When he was younger, he'd make me cards, and draw pictures for me to display on the refrigerator. At school, he'd make ornaments at Christmas and hide them under the Christmas tree, anxious and excited for me to open them everyday until Christmas.

As he got older, he was only excited about what was underneath the Christmas tree for him. Of course, I would get a "Happy Birthday Mom", or a "Happy Mother's Day", but this was the first time in years that I had received a tangible object from my child.

I was nervous about my blood pressure. I was too young to have a stroke or heart attack. I was only 38 years old. I had no warning signs… other than the headaches I had been experiencing for two weeks. I just thought it was stress. I thought I had done well with not letting things bother me. I believed I had a handle on the way life's issues weighed on me. I was wrong. Blood pressure readings of 185 over 120 told a different story.

I prayed about the situation, and went on. What good was worrying going to do, right? As my pastor used to say, "worry never paid a bill, so why worry?" But I was worrying. On the inside. I thought I had dealt with my son being in jail. I had cried about it for an hour, felt pain in my heart for a month, yet I was determined to remind myself that I wasn't the cause of his behavior, his probation violation for being caught with marijuana. I was determined to make myself believe that because he was an adult, people wouldn't blame me for his mistakes. They would know that his choices were his, and his alone.

The day before Mother's Day, he called me. He had been a little worried because he hadn't been able to get in touch with me.

"Mama, what's up? Where you been? I been calling you." he said with worry in his voice.

"I was in the hospital." I told him.

Silence was momentary. "In the hospital? For what? What's wrong?" he asked.

I explained to him about my blood pressure and how I was taking medicine, and being monitored by my doctor.

"Wow. I can't believe I'm in here. And you are sick. Anything could happen to you…" He was quiet. Then he told me he loved me. I could hear sadness in his voice. "I'm going to be different when I get out of here. You'll see. I should be there, taking care of you…not here. You'll see."

As soon as I opened my eyes Mother's Day, my eyes fell on the card on my nightstand. I sat up, reached for the card, looked at it, and sighed. When I opened the card, I found a personal note inside that said:

Dear Mom;
I've seen a lot of women, and have yet to meet a woman as strong, intelligent and respectable as you are. I pray that you forgive me for my lack of respect and appreciation for all the love and sacrifices you made throughout my lifetime for me to be happy. I'm turning over a new leaf when I get out so I can redeem myself and make you proud of me like I am of you.

Tears ran down my face. It was the most beautiful thing I had read in a long time.

As the weeks went on, I visited my son as often as I could. He talked about his future. He talked about praying for himself. He talked about being a role model for the young kids that looked up to him. He talked about getting tattoos, and about the gangs that were inside the jail. He talked about books that he had read during his free time, and about playing basketball and working out. He spoke about the food, and how he couldn't wait to get real food when he got out.

I wondered what he would be like when he did get out; if the experience would make him a better man, or a bitter man. I had read how people who spend time in jail become reformed or transformed.

One of my favorite books, "*A Lesson Before Dying*" by Ernest Gaines, had impressed upon me the importance of a man who was on death row dying with dignity and as a man by learning to read, and being able to tell others that he was a human being, rather than a hog, as he was called by the lawyer who represented him.

I cried during portions of the book. I wondered what it would be like to go through life not knowing how to read. I thought how awful it must be to go through life unable to go to the bathroom in privacy, living behind bars, unable to go to the refrigerator and choose what I wanted. How unbelievable it must be to have someone orchestrating your day, and most certainly, wearing the same colors every day. It was those same thoughts that went through my mind as I thought about my child, as grown as he was. Although he was highly intelligent, and knew how to read, and wasn't on death row, he had little privacy, was living behind bars, was unable to sleep in his own bed, unable to go to the refrigerator and drink up as much Kool-aid and tea as he wanted, or eat up all of the chips, leaving the crumbs in the bag for someone to find; he wore the same orange and white jump suit everyday, and he had to go by the schedule created for him by the system.

Each time I visited the jail, I told myself, "not much longer". It was a dreary place. It was a sad place. I watched parents, spouses, siblings, children and friends waiting to see their loved ones. I could hear conversations going on between them and the inmates.

On one visit, I heard a lady dressed in a mini skirt and halter top with red scraggly hair, explaining to her boyfriend that she was sorry that she had hurt him. She stated that she didn't want the guy that he caught her with. She just wanted things between them to work out. She told him she had gone to the clinic to make sure she was clean, and wanted him to know that she loved him.

I heard another man in scrubs talking to his brother about financial affairs.

One lady, visiting her boyfriend, was talking about the latest drama in their lives, dealing with exes, and child support issues.

Another lady talked to her son about being safe and making positive choices. I smiled as I heard her because she sounded like me.

One lady cried as she shared the news of the passing of a loved one with the person she was visiting.

Another young lady smiled as she showed her new born baby to his imprisoned father for the first time.

I was so sad inside. I hated that place. I hated what it stood for. I hated how it made me feel, embarrassed for having to go there. While others walked into the building laughing and smiling, I saw no reason to smile or laugh. That was JAIL! A facility that housed criminals. People who had broken the law in many different ways were housed there. As a mother, I was not proud to be seen walking into the building. As a person, I was not happy to know that my offspring, my child, my baby, was locked up there. As a Christian, I was saddened to know that I had somehow failed to pray hard enough to keep my child on the right path. As a woman, I recalled how people categorized men who had been in jail. As an employer, I knew it would be hard for my son to be a productive member of society because he had been in jail, and employers don't particularly like to hire individuals who have been in jail. My son wasn't a murderer, or a rapist, or a thief, but to have to write on a job application that he had been arrested for possession of marijuana would raise a negative red flag with most, if not all employers who ran across his job application.

One day, while I was relaxing, trying to get my blood pressure down, I got a text message from one of his friends saying he had called them collect and said he had gotten into a fight. My heart was racing. He wasn't in a place where I could just call and check on him. He wasn't in a place where I could just drive over and see if he was ok. He was in jail. I was determined to not let this get to me. I prayed for him, just as I did several times a day. I knew that he would be alright.

One night, several weeks after my son was arrested, I received a phone call from a close friend. She asked how I was doing and told me that she wanted me to know that it wasn't my fault that my son was in jail. She told me not to let it worry me, and not to make myself sick about it. I told her that in my heart, I knew that I didn't teach my son to make bad choices. I knew that parents could only teach their children so much, but it was ultimately the child's choice to make. I told her that my child knew right from wrong. He knew that I prayed for him everyday, and he had even told me once that he knew the only reason why he was still alive was because his mother prayed for him. He even knew how to pray for himself.

After I got off the phone with her, I thought back to conversations I had with my son on different occasions. Whenever he was worried about something, he would call and say he needed to see me. He had to talk to me. I would wait for him to arrive, and I would sit at the kitchen table for hours, as he sat at the kitchen counter, eating everything in site, and drinking glass after glass of Kool-aid. I would listen to him say what was on his mind. I would allow him to vent, and confess. I would sit, not judging, not fussing, not argumentative, and allow him to share what was on his heart. In his mind, even though he didn't always make the best choices, he knew that he had been taught what was right.

I recall smiling to myself, as he stated some of the most obvious things that I hadn't realized he paid attention to.

On one occasion, my son shared with me how he appreciated the fact that he had never had to experience what it was like to not have electricity or heat at home. He expressed how terrible it was to be at his friend's house, and the gas had been turned off in the middle of winter. He expressed gratitude for me paying the bills so that he didn't have to experience that in his own home.

On another occasion, my son thanked me for making him do his homework and go to school because he knew how important it was to know how to read and write. He had friends who had a hard time in school, and he was glad that he was encouraged in the area of education.

He surprised me one night while explaining how a friend's mother had made a pass at him. Even more surprising was the fact that he had paid attention to me as an individual, not just as his mother, saying that he was proud that he had a mother that didn't jump from man to man, and that he was glad that my mother had raised me to be able to take care of myself. He was proud that his mother wasn't dependent on somebody to take care of her.

As parents, we don't really know what our children think of us. I knew my son thought I was the meanest mother in the world when he had a curfew and his friends didn't. I knew he asked God once why did he have to get stuck with me for a mother. He wanted to know if he could get a mother who was nice, and didn't have rules. I laugh when I think of that prayer request. To know that he had acknowledged some of the simplest things, made me smile inside. I recalled receiving several phone calls from him, simply requesting me to pray for him. Those were nights that I didn't sleep.

Every night when I lay down to rest, I ask God to keep my child safe. I ask him to guide him in the right direction, and help him make good choices.

I got a call several months after receiving that sad call from my son. This one was different. He had happiness in his voice, rather than sadness. He was being released from jail.

You want to know who I am? I am a determined mother who won't stop praying for her child, because I know that the prayers of the righteous avails much. It is because of my determination that my son is a more mature young man who is making better choices, because he has a mother who prays for him.

THE LOVE OF MY LIFE

I am, a no nonsense type of person. I studied hard in school, worked hard on any job I had, and took life seriously. I didn't allow just anyone to get close to me, but especially to my heart. As a matter of fact, I only dated a few guys in my life. One of whom was the love of my life.

I was working and going to college. I didn't have much time for a social life. Yet I knew when I met the love of my life that I would have no doubt who he was. You see, I had this list. A long list of what I was looking for in a man. I'm not the only one. Most women create a list; some keep it in their heads, others write it down on paper. I carried mine in my heart, the place where love grows. So, it took a while for me to meet my "Mr. Right for *Me*". I wasn't even looking for him. I had friends and family trying to hook me up. But I was not interested.

Not long after I graduated from college and began teaching, I attended a party at a friend's house. While mingling with the people, many of whom I didn't know, my eyes became fixated on this beautiful beige colored man with the most intense hazel colored eyes. I guess his eyes were fixated too, because he was watching me, watch him. Not usually one to stare, I diverted my attention elsewhere. But a few minutes later, he came over and introduced himself to me. He was tall, and handsome. He was a gentleman. He was intelligent and extremely sexy. And, he was trying to rap to me! Of all the women in the room, some dressed to impress, some who had been throwing themselves at him, and he was trying to talk to me. I laugh every time I think of that day. The day which turned into night, and the next morning, because we spent hours getting to know each other. We *talked* all night, and before we left each other the next day, he told me that I was going to be his wife. I laughed. Pretty cocky for someone who had just met me. But, I will admit, I could see the possibility and potential of that happening. I liked everything about him. The fact that we had spent the night together, just talking, was so impressive. Most men would have been trying to have sex. But that was the farthest thing on our minds. We just got to know each other. By the time we left each other the next day, I knew his whole life story, and he knew mine. I knew his plans for the future, his likes and dislikes, his fears and hopes and dreams. And, he knew mine as well.

We talked on the phone later that day and into the night. He was a military man, and was stationed nearby. So, every night that we were away from each other, we talked each other to sleep.

I was in love with him. I loved his heart, his mind, his thoughts, his gentleness, his conversation, his intellect, his sense of humor, his laugh, his whole being. He told me things that made me know he loved me too. He thought I was beautiful. He asked me how my day was. He tended to my needs, and cared about my thoughts. He made love to me mentally and emotionally, everyday, without even being in the same room with me.

It wasn't long before we were talking marriage. I knew he was the man I was meant to marry. God sent him to me. God put all the qualities that I had written in my heart that I desired in the man that was just right for me into this beautiful creation that desired to be apart of my life.

After we were married, we went through the typical "getting to know your way of doing things" that most married couples do. Because we didn't live together prior to marriage, we weren't aware of each others habits. It's funny. I was so predictable and set in my own way of doing things. And he had his way of doing things. For instance, I had always done the laundry on the weekend. But my new husband liked to do the laundry in the middle of the week so that our weekends were free of housework. Being independent by nature, I fought with him over the way we handled our finances. Yet, because of his smooth talk, and calm demeanor, I was able to see that his way of doing a lot of things was actually more efficient. That's what love does. It allows you to see things through your lover's eyes, and shows you trust. Trust and dependability you never knew before, beyond your parents. Love, respect, trust. He was my best friend. He was the love of my life. And I was determined to spend every day that God gave me loving this man, and appreciating the fact that God thought enough of me, to put him in my life.

My husband spoiled me. He cooked dinner, did house work. Ironed my clothes! Whatever I needed, or wanted, he made sure I had it. He was my king. I was his queen. Eventually, I found out we were going to have a little princess. I smile as I think about it.

When my daughter was born, we had the perfect life. We lived in Germany for a while, because he had been stationed there for a tour of duty.

We were so happy. When we came back to the States, we bought a beautiful home, and planned to live happily ever after.

Then one day, heartache knocked on our door. My husband had been diagnosed with cancer. Because he was such a strong person, we vowed to think positively about our situation. He followed the doctor's orders. He took medicines. He went through treatments. All while maintaining a positive attitude.

I prayed for my husband every time I thought about him. Anything I could do to make him comfortable, I did it. While still trying to be a mother, a teacher and a rock for my husband, I had to encourage myself at times. I didn't want to think of having a life without the man that God had given me, my soul mate. I didn't want to think of raising our daughter without her father. I didn't want to think of him not seeing her graduate from high school, or walking her down the aisle at her wedding. So, I pushed all those thoughts aside, and focused on the positives. I was determined to show the love of my life that this was just a stumbling block. We were going to be ok. He was going to be ok. Our family, our life, everything we were working towards together, was going to be ok.

God had a different plan. Although I didn't understand why he would give me such happiness, only to sprinkle it with sadness, I had to deal with watching my love walk through the valley of the shadow of death. I was walking with him. However, I was going to come out on this side, while he was slowly walking into the light.

There were tubes hooked up. There were machines and lights and sounds going off. The room was cold and sad. My husband was surrounded by nurses and doctors. I was there too, praying and trying to understand what the doctors were saying. Tears were forming in my eyes. I didn't want him to see me cry. My heart was aching, but I had to be strong for him. I had to be strong for our daughter, too.

"Oh, God! Please don't let this be happening!" As I sat in his room, I began to talk to God. And, God, began to talk back. God told me that everything was going to be fine. God had shown me what true love was, and allowed me to experience it, so that I could give it. God told me that

He had given me the characteristics of a strong women, so that I could be ready for this day when it came. God told me that He was not punishing me, but that He was blessing my husband by giving him rest. The cancer was causing his body to be in pain, and my husband needed rest. God promised to take care of me and my daughter. God promised that He would comfort me when I needed it the most, and that every time I looked into my daughter's eyes, I would see my husband because she looked just like him.

Sadly, the day came when it was time to say goodbye to the love of my life. The doctors had done all that they were capable of doing and God had chosen to bring my husband's young life to an end.

I remember the nurse telling me that she was going to turn off the machines and unhook the tubes that had helped my husband sustain life for just a little longer. With tears in my eyes, I kissed my husband, said goodbye, and lovingly and carefully unhooked the tubes myself. It was my job, my duty as his wife to care for him as his life came to a prideful and triumphant end, just as I had cared for him in his healthy and strong moments of our lives together. For a while, after my love took his last breath, I sat there still holding his hand, watching him. I was still connected to him. As his heart stopped beating, I thought mine would stop too. I loved him, and the fact that he was no longer with me physically would not change the mental and emotional bond I had formed with him.

My daughter and I are fine. I remind her often of how wonderful her father was and how much he loved her. I share with her small glimpses of his plans for her. She has memories of him that I didn't imagine she could have. I thought she was too young to remember him. She amazes me sometimes when she says, "I remember when Dad…"

I miss my love dearly. I think of him every day. I see his memory in the furniture we chose together, in the wedding ring I still wear. I hear his voice when I feel alone, or when I have a stressful day. I can see his smile when my daughter smiles…see his loving eyes when I look into my daughter's eyes. I am reminded of him when I do the laundry on Wednesday and when I hear our favorite song.

I am certain that I will never find another love like my husband. I am determined to not let his legacy vanish from my memory.

God has a way of giving us just what we need when we need it…and He heals our broken hearts with time. He holds us and comforts us in our saddest moments, and assures us that everything will be just fine.

I believe that I was truly blessed when I met my husband, and the small dose of sorrow that I have experienced is minimal compared to the joy I have been blessed to experience.

My advice to others is, be determined to love the love of your life. Don't get caught up in minor things that keep you frustrated and angry. Love each other, appreciate each other, laugh with each other, trust each other, pray for each other, and be determined to make every day seem as important as the day you married each other.

SANTA IS REAL

When I was little, I loved Christmas. I loved the pretty lights, the decorations, the Christmas tree, the music, the presents, the story of Jesus' birth, and the Christmas movies that came on TV. I loved everything about Christmas.

I remember writing letters to Santa Claus, and asking for baby dolls Barbie dolls, clothes, Barbie dream houses, Barbie automobiles, games, and sometimes a bike. My favorite animal when I was a child was the monkey, so for several years, I asked Santa to bring me a monkey for Christmas.

Every Christmas morning, I would get up bright and early, and run into the living room to see what Santa left for me. Although there was no lively, hairy monkey sitting in a cage underneath the Christmas tree, there was everything that I asked Santa for, including a stuffed monkey, along with a note from Santa for me to be a good girl, and mind my parents.

My cousins and I used to have debates about whether or not Santa was real. My mom had always told me that if you believe in Santa, then he was real. If you didn't believe in Santa, then, he wasn't real.

I listened to my cousins with their philosophies about how could Santa fly all over the world in one night, and deliver gifts to so many kids.

I listened to one cousin complain about how she had asked Santa for a particular item for Christmas, and Santa didn't bring it. Needless to say, she was angry with Santa.

I had no qualms with Santa, because anything I had ever put on my list, I got it.

One year, I proved to my cousins that Santa was real. I told them that Santa was going to bring me a bike, and that I hadn't told my parents about it so they were going to be surprised too. I was determined to prove to them that Santa was real.

My mother happened to overhear our argument, because my cousins and I had been sitting at the kitchen table. I imagine, that since it was only a few days before Christmas, and I had not told my mother that Santa was bringing me a bike, she and my father had to revise their plans so that Santa could deliver my bike to me on Christmas morning.

My family spent every other Christmas in Oklahoma with my mother's family, and Santa had never had a problem finding me or leaving me what was on my Christmas list.

For some strange reason that year, my parents had to borrow a truck with a camper on it to drive to Oklahoma. My mom had told me that we had too many Christmas presents to take with us, so they needed more room than our two door Pontiac would hold.

I didn't care. All I knew was that Santa was bringing me a bike, and I was going to prove to my cousins that he was real!

Just as always, when I woke up that morning, Santa had come! And, he had left me a shiny new red bike. I couldn't wait to get back home, and show my cousins my new bike. They were amazed to find out that Santa had brought my bike all the way to Oklahoma.

Years later, when I was in junior high school, I knew the truth about Santa Claus, but I never brought it up. I enjoyed pretending, just as my parents did, that Santa would mysteriously climb down our chimney every year and leave me presents by our Christmas tree.

My eighth grade year, my parents asked me what I wanted Santa to bring me for Christmas. I told them I wanted a real monkey that year, and a ten-speed bike.

That Christmas Eve, after I had gone to sleep, I was awaken by voices. As I listened, I could hear my mom, dad, and one of my uncles in the kitchen. I could hear them reading the directions to something. Then, I could hear the sound of tools hitting the floor. I could hear the sound of confusion, as something hadn't been put on right, and had to be taken off again. Then I heard the sound a bicycle makes when you change its speeds. They were putting together my bike!

I smiled to myself, as I heard my Santa Claus and his elves trying to figure things out. I found myself laughing when I heard my mother tell them to be quiet because I was going to hear them. Immediately, they quieted down.

I woke up the next morning, and went into the leaving room, just as I had done every year since I was two-years old on Christmas morning.

There was my shiny new, blue ten-speed bike, with a bow on it, and my stuffed monkey.

I never did tell my parents that I heard them in the kitchen that night. I hated to ruin the fun. But for every Christmas that my mother was alive, no matter how old I was, Santa always left something special for me by the tree on Christmas morning.

I still love Christmas, and I have always been just as determined to make Christmas as special for my children, as my parents made it for me.

So, every Christmas morning, my children, and grandchildren will find something special by the tree, with their name on it, and a note from Santa. Although my children are old enough to know the truth about Santa, they are determined to maintain some of the special moments from their childhood years. They wake up early on Christmas morning, just like I did, and go into the living room to see if Santa left them what they asked for.

I am determined to pass down special, memorable traditions to my children that my parents passed down to me. It is my hope that they will pass this special, memorable tradition down to their children, no matter what others may say or think, because it was something special to their grandmother.

INTERPRETATIONS

From the day we are born, until the day our place on this earth comes to end, we are hypnotized with the word love. When we are born, it is hopefully something that smothers us. As we grow, it is a word spoken daily to us, hopefully by our parents and grandparents. As we grow older, it is something that we come to understand and therefore carry in our hearts.

As we become wiser by the days, through living life's constant whirlwind of emotions, love captures us, disappoints us, embraces us, drains us, brings us joy and sorrow, regret and doubt. Love makes us soar and dream, it fulfills us and consumes us. It makes us glow, and can just as easily make us feel gloomy. Love is the sun and the rainbow. It is peace and pleasantness.

Love is found in a smile, and through a touch. It is heard in words spoken and seen through the sparkle in one's eyes. Love is a lifeline, an IV unit that keeps us nourished. It is a beverage that quenches our thirst for emotional attachment. It is the air we breathe. Love is in the little things we do for others, that shows how much we care.

Love is sharing, caring, feeling, believing, connecting, non-judgmental, forgiving, emotional, time consuming, worth the effort and imperfect.

Love is uncontrollable, because it comes from the heart, where it is born, where it lives, where it grows, where it receives what it needs to survive.

Love is unavoidable. We all have received it and given it. We all have felt it and yearned for it. And even found it hard to walk away from when we knew it was hurting us, destroying us. Love hurts, although in fairy tales, it doesn't. Fairy tales; the place where love lives happily ever after.

For me, love began with my parent's hugs and affection when I was little. Love came through in the words they spoke, which made me feel secure. Love for me was my mother singing me to sleep at night. It was her tending to my bloody knees when I fell off my bike. Love for me was the special Big Red floats my mother made for me in the special ice cream glass. Love was joining my mother for a cup of coffee, of which my cup contained more sugar than coffee, at night while we watched TV.

Love for me was my dad dancing to music while holding me close to his heart and smiling. Love for me was hearing my dad tell me often that I was beautiful and smart, and that I had natural beauty, so I didn't need to mess it up with makeup.

Love for me was receiving letters in the mail from my grandmother who lived in Oklahoma. Sometimes there would be money inside, but most of the time it was just a letter in very distinct handwriting, encouraging me to be good and reminding me she loved me.

Love for me was eating a bowl of vanilla ice cream at night with my grandfather, during the summer. He loved ice cream so much, he wiggled his toes while he ate it.

Love for me was going to 7-11 Corner Store with my other grandfather to get a Slurpee. He was so nice, he let me and my cousins get the big one!

Love is like a finely cut jewel. Despite it's many facets, love is truly priceless, and best experienced when it's given and received in the same way.

It is my determination to receive the blessing of love that God has for me, no matter what type of past experiences I have had with love. It may not come in the form of a mate. However, it comes in so many subtle forms, that you have to pay attention, or you may miss them.

Like, when my granddaughter noticed my toenails were polished purple. And she squatted down and touched my big toe, then looked up at me, and back down, and touched her big toe. That was sign language for "do mine too!" I gladly got the purple toe nail polish, and the cotton balls and polish remover and spent an hour polishing and fixing the tiny toe nails of a little princess, who after all my hard work, was so excited to show off her toes to anyone she saw.

Like, when my godson, who visits me in the summer hugs me every time he sees me, even if it has only been ten minutes since the last time he saw me, or comes and sits beside me and lays his head on my arm.

Like, when my godson has to go home, and lets me know that he won't forget me and can't wait to come back the next time.

Like, when the little boy who sees his mom after a long day, greets her with, "How was your day Mom?" and makes her smile.

Like, when my Pastor eulogized his beloved wife. His love and pain working together to create an amazing memorial in celebration of her life, and their lives together. A story, only a loving, devoted husband could share, as his hurting heart beat with a little less enthusiasm.

Like, when a sister who is struggling with cancer finds the strength to smile at family and friends, as hard as it may be.

Like, when a best friend bakes your favorite cake just because she knows you are coming for a visit.

Like, when a daughter takes her mother to breakfast just because she wants to spend time with her.

Like, when a father sits in the cold and rain, watching his son play football, disregarding the weather, or his runny nose, and cold feet.

Like, when a parent goes without buying things for themselves, so that their children don't have to go without.

Like, when a stranger sees a homeless person and gives them food to eat.

Like, when a neighbor takes another neighbor to the store, just because she knows that she has no ride of her own.

Like, when family and friends rally around a loved one who is transitioning from this life, and taking the journey to the valley of the shadow of death.

I am determined to share love, to be loved and be open to the love that God has for me.

And now abideth faith, hope and love; these three, but the greatest of these is love.

THE BEAT DOWN

Oh my gosh!!!!! I just couldn't believe it! Never in a million years would I have thought it would happen in my house, with my child.

I mean, we talked. I was open with her about sex. She's just a kid. Only 14! Way too young to think she knows what's best for her.

I should have paid attention. I should have seen the signs. Hmmm. I don't know. I guess I had blinders on, and not just on my eyes, but my mind too.

That time when I read those graphic text messages from the boy, asking her to do sexual things with him, I should have not given the cell phone back. I can't be with her all the time. I, just thought she was making better choices.

She was getting in trouble at school. I thought it was typical. She was a teenager who wanted to be the class clown. She was always trying to get attention. I grounded her, but it didn't help. I took away phone privileges. It worked for awhile.

Then, she was missing after school one day. No one knew where she was. After about an hour, she called me. When questioned about where she had been, she claimed that I must have forgotten that she told me she had detention after school. I thought I was losing my mind. I try to remember things that are important. That day seemed to repeat itself over and over. To put a stop to it, I began making arrangements to have her picked up at a certain time everyday. Problem solved. I was determined to nip things in the bud with my teenager, and believed that I had. But she had a different type of determination brewing inside of her.

That day had been just like any other day. Crazy! Work was crazy,

29

the kids were crazy, and I think my husband and I were acting crazy with each other. Then, the phone call came; news that crushed my heart into small pieces.

As I slowly drove home, to deal with the issue that had come to me via a cell phone call, I cried. "What is wrong with me?" I questioned. "What did I do wrong?" "How could this have happened?" "O, God! Please help me deal with this in a calm manner." I was far from calm. I was enraged. My heart was pounding inside my chest. I was going over in my mind what I would say when I confronted her. I wanted to be rational.

Was this really the appropriate time to be rational? I thought about it for a few minutes, and then convinced myself that I would be as rational as possible.

That only lasted about as long as it took me to get in the house. As soon as I saw her, I became enraged. My husband was there. We were both furious with her. She, however, had no idea that I knew the secret she had been keeping from us. She had been walking around like nothing had happened, like she had done nothing wrong.

My heart was pounding. As I looked at my husband, I could see his veins popping out of his forehead. That handsome face that I loved to look at, held no smile or warmth. It was unreadable and sad.

We sat her in the living room. Not really knowing where to begin. Her demeanor upset me more and more, as she acted like she had no reason to be sitting there, because we had interrupted her favorite show, and made her hang up the phone while she was on an important call.

Before my husband could reach out, and touch her, I asked her was there anything she wanted to tell us. She said no, but was looking a little nervous. "Are you sure," I asked. "Because you may want to tell me your version of what I already know." She just looked at me, pretending not to have a clue to what I was referring to.

My husband piped in. "Do you want to tell us what happened to the window screen in your room?"

Several nights before, my daughter had cut the screen from her bedroom window, and crawled out of it in the wee hours of the morning. She had gotten in the car with a boy she barely knew, and went somewhere to have unprotected sex with him. She then climbed back in the window of her bedroom, washed herself off, and went to bed.

It didn't take long for the boy to start bragging about what he had done with my daughter. As luck would have it, one of the people he told, knew somebody who knew me. Imagine my disbelief and disappointment. I couldn't breath. I thought my heart would stop.

My daughter, after being confronted with what we knew, didn't deny anything. And, needless to say, I tried to kill her! I know it was God that kept me from beating her to death.

My husband nailed her window shut, and took the hinges off the door to her room. I took her cell phone, and anything that seemed like a privilege.

I can't believe her! I can't believe what she did! I can't believe she put herself, her life, her health in jeopardy! Anything could have happened to her. He could have killed her. She could have been raped. She could have been gang raped. She could have gotten pregnant. Well, luckily for me, I had the since to have her put on the pill a month before. I am glad I did. What if she caught something from him? A disease! Or, worse, HIV or AIDS!

I remember praying and asking God to not let her be pregnant. I remember praying to God to not let her have some dreadful disease. I remember asking God how to make this situation right. I remember thinking and wondering what would make my daughter do such a thing. I thought back to indicators that were clues that my daughter might have been teetering on the verge of some terrible act of insaneness such as sneaking out to have sex.

I was devastated because we had talked openly about not having sex because it was something that should be experienced with someone you love, someone special, someone you are married to.

My decision to put her on the pill was something I had thought about for months. It wasn't an easy decision for me because I didn't want her to think I was giving her permission to have sex. Yet, I have to admit that I didn't want any surprises, with her coming to me and saying she thought she was pregnant. I was determined to prevent my daughter from becoming a mother prematurely.

Several days later, I sat her down to have another talk. I told her that I was disappointed in her and that I never thought she would have made such a choice. I told her that she had basically tainted herself, and was now damaged goods. I told her I loved her, but that I didn't trust her, and that it would be a long time before I would be able to trust her again.

I cry when I think of how my daughter was being talked about by some little boy who had taken her virginity. I wondered what other adults would say when they heard what she had done.

I only shared my painful story of my daughter's unbelievable foolishness with a handful of people. Each of whom encouraged me to not blame myself for what happened. One reminded me that I made the best choice I could have when I had her put on the pill.

I am a good parent.

I am a loving parent.

I am a nurturing parent.

I am a determined parent.

I am determined to figure out a way to help my daughter realize the beauty of herself, encompass the essence of who she is, encourage her belief in accountability, make her learn the importance of trustworthiness, desire to know the difference between love and sex, and more importantly, help her find within herself the self-esteem quality that makes her love herself so much, that nothing and no one can break that spirit that makes her know and believe that she is important and deserving of a great future, that doesn't include unprotected sex with boys, or men, who don't care about her mentally, emotionally or spiritually, only physically and sexually.

I know I am not the only parent who is going through something with her teenage daughter, however I believe that the determination I have to find a way to get through to my daughter, will make the difference in her choices. I won't stop paying attention to what she does, or says, or who she hangs out with. I won't stop checking her phone, reading her text messages or eavesdropping on her phone calls. I won't stop reading the notes that I find lying around in her room, because these are the clues that give parents answers when they have nagging feelings. Some people may say that it is an invasion of her privacy, but I believe that too much privacy can lead to big problems.

I am determined to make it through my daughter's teen years gracefully and prayerfully.

ANGELS UNAWARE

I am a pretty observant person. The people I notice most are the quiet ones because they kind of stand out. I try to treat all people the same, no matter who they are. My mom once told me that you should befriend kings, homeless people, and everyone in between. She said that we should treat them all alike because they are all people. God's people.

The Bible talked about that in Hebrews 13:2, where we are encouraged to *Be not forgetful to entertain strangers: for thereby some have entertained angels unawares.* I take that scripture to heart because it is encouraging us to treat others kindly, regardless of how they look, or how we perceive them to be, because you never know what testimonials God has planted in our midst. Sometimes all we have to do is just speak or smile, just show a little human kindness and something amazing can happen.

By nature we are skeptical of getting close to strangers. We look at them, and wonder what their life is like; what they are thinking about as they sit quietly, thinking to themselves.

One day, a tall, thin, dark-skinned man walked into the building I worked in. He didn't say much. He was there to work, to clean our building. And that's what he did. I observed him on many occasions, working with his head down, walking with his head down. I thought about that mentality that many older people grew up with when dealing with supervisors, keep your head down and your mouth shut. Don't start no trouble, won't be no trouble. Sort of like the slave mentality that kept so many alive during the slave period and the Civil Rights era.

He was there for several weeks before I learned his name. By chance, he had received a phone call, and the person who answered our office phones that day told the caller that there was no one in our building by that name,

Mr. Wilson. The caller called again. Angry this time. So, as I was the one who happened to answer the call, the woman was irate. As I calmed her down long enough to understand what she wanted, she explained who she was looking for. Although I did not know the strangers name, I took it upon myself to go find him and ask him what his name was. He looked at me and said, *"Mr. Wilson."*

Each day that followed, I made it a point to speak to *Mr. Wilson.* His voice was soft and scraggly at the same time because there was something wrong with his throat. As he spoke, he would have to take his hand and push his vocal chords to make them work. The first time I saw him do this, my heart ached. I'm a cry baby, sentimental type. So, to see this man having to make an extra effort to do something I take for granted everyday, to be able to just open my mouth and speak or scream or laugh, I was abundantly thankful to God at that moment. Silently, I asked God to bless this man. Whatever his situation or circumstance was, all I could think to do was ask God to bless him.

As the weeks past, I found myself enraged one day by a coworker who was being rude to Mr. Wilson. For one, she wasn't taking the time to understand what he was asking her, and secondly, she was treating him as though he was beneath her. I noticed his frustration, and asked him what he needed. I listened for a few minutes and then helped him with what he was trying to do.

I was brought up to respect my elders. It is my observation that some people believe that just because they dress better than someone else, or look better than someone else, or make more money than someone else, they can look down on them and maybe unknowingly, mistreat them. However, our elders are our elders and respect is always due.

One day as I was driving down the street not far from my job, I saw Mr. Wilson walking. It was 103 degrees outside, but he was walking like he didn't have a care in the world. He wasn't walking hurriedly. Just walking. I wondered where he was walking to and if he had family. I tried to guess his age. Thought he might be in his sixties, maybe his seventies. He was so thin, I wondered did he eat properly.

I thought about a book I had read once. It was one of those books that just kind of sticks with you and makes you recall certain passages from time to time. It was a book about a white rich man and a black homeless man who had become friends over a period of time. The rich man's wife had been a volunteer at a homeless shelter and urged her husband to start volunteering at the shelter. The homeless man was quiet, reserved and untrusting. So when the rich man made an attempt to get to know him, he pushed him away. After awhile, and many attempts by the rich man to befriend the homeless man, the rich man expressed his desire to be friends. The homeless man thought over the proposition of friendship with this rich white man, with whom he undoubtedly had nothing in common. He told him that he wasn't sure if he could be his friend because he didn't want to be like the fish people catch and release back into the water, just to be able to say they caught a fish. He explained to the rich man that if that was what he was looking for, to be able to say he was friends with a homeless man, and then they go their separate ways and live their separate lives, he wanted no parts of it. However, if he wanted a friend, a true friend, then he would be his friend, despite their differences. Amazingly, the rich man eventually took the homeless man into his home and even gave him a job. The former homeless man prayed for the rich man's wife who was ill. He maintained a prayer vigil and because of it was able to create a powerful bond with that family. The wife died, sadly, but the two men, the rich man and the poor man, maintained a strong bond that became more like a family bond than a friendship bond. After reading that book, I began to see homeless people and people down on their luck in a different light. We never know what a person has been through to get them to the place they happen to be in life. Amazingly, we don't have to know. It isn't our business. But, if we are truly Christians, and practicing God's examples, we can be about the business of sisterly and brotherly love.

One day, as I was sitting in my office, I noticed that Mr. Wilson was wearing a shirt that he had on earlier in the week. I don't know what made me notice, but I did. So, I called home and told my son to go through his closet and find some nice shirts that he no longer wanted. I then called a coworker who seemed to be about the same size as Mr. Wilson and asked him if he had any shirts that he no longer needed. I explained to him that I was trying to anonymously give these clothes to Mr. Wilson in hopes that he wouldn't be offended by the gesture. Several days later, my coworker dropped off some nice, expensive shirts to my office. That reminded me of something I heard my Pastor say in church, that you don't give something to someone that you wouldn't wear yourself. I thought to myself, "Mr. Wilson is going to be sharp in these shirts!"

After getting a few coworkers to place the clothing items in Mr. Wilson's work area, I noticed that Mr. Wilson had a sad look on his face. The next day, he approached me and said, in his soft scraggly voice, "Thank you very much for the clothes." Then he turned his head. I think he had tears in his eyes, but I didn't want to find out for sure. The intent was to help. Not embarrass or sadden. I looked him in his eyes and told him he was welcome. And I walked away.

The next day, when the building seemed to be quiet and empty, and I had my head down, trying to figure out something on the computer, I saw a figure out of the corner of my left eye standing in the doorway. Quietly, standing there. Waiting for me to look up and address him. It was Mr. Wilson.

"Hey Mr. Wilson," I said.

He looked at me and replied, "I just want you to know that I think you are a beautiful person, beautiful on the inside for thinking of me, and beautiful on the outside too. I don't talk too much, but I notice people, and I knew you were beautiful, had a beautiful spirit, even before you did what you did."

Of course I was blushing, as I explained to him that I was just glad that I could help.

As he began to wear his new shirts, I noticed a little spunk in Mr. Wilson. He would walk a little taller, smile a little more often and hold his head up higher than before. Just to make sure that I wasn't trying to see something that wasn't there, I asked another coworker if they had noticed a change in Mr. Wilson. He agreed that there indeed had been a transformation in his behavior for the better. I smiled to myself, as I realized that just one small act of kindness can have multiple affects on an individual.

One day Mr. Wilson came in my office and sat down. "How are you today?" I asked.

"I'm doing alright." He asked me about the pictures on my wall, and made small talk. I in turn asked him if he had lived in the City all of his life. He explained how he was from another state and had gotten in trouble with the law, had been to prison and was now paroled to the City. I was shocked when he told me he would be on parole until 2044. He shook his head in disbelief as he stated, "paroled for armed robbery. I didn't even have a weapon. But I will be on parole until I die."

My body language never changed. I didn't look at him differently. Just told him that it was good that he was getting the chance to make a change and I wished him the best. He went on to explain how cancer ran in his family, and how his father, and mother and sister also had cancer at some point. I can't recall which, but one of his parents had died from it. So, he wasn't letting the fact that it was hereditary and also had caught up to him hold him to a negative place.

I worked with Mr. Wilson a little while longer. I learned many things by watching this thin, fragile man, who said little but observed much. Who heard much, but commented on nothing. Just working to make a living, and dealing with his past that would never let him forget his mistakes.

All my life, I had been determined to help people when I could. I had been determined not to look down on others because they were different, or act afraid because they weren't like me. I wasn't ignorant, I paid attention to what was going on, and resolved to not put myself in situations that could do me harm. But I believe that when God placed Mr. Wilson in my building, and made me take notice of him, He placed an Angel in my midst.

You see, there was a lot of tension in the building in which I worked. Whenever Mr. Wilson would come stand by my office, or speak to me with his soft scraggly voice, I felt a calmness. I recall that as Mr. Wilson sat in my office that day and confessed that he had been to prison, it didn't bother me. It didn't scare me. It made me respect him even more. I felt as though I entertained an Angel unaware, and that my determination to do God's will by showing love towards Mr. Wilson, allowed me to receive that peace that surpasses understanding throughout my day. Thank you God for my Angel, in the form of Mr. Wilson.

DON'T WORRY, BE HAPPY

I am a single mother who worked hard to put herself through college. Life wasn't easy for me growing up, so I made sure that my children didn't have to experience any of the hardships and disappointments that I did.

I encouraged my children to be the best that they could be in life. I encouraged them to love themselves, even if no one else did. I encouraged them to see the beauty in themselves, even if no one else did. I encouraged them to laugh at life, even if it was hard to.

Life is too short to be sad, or depressed. Life is too full of possibilities for us not to grab hold of opportunities.

I am a happy person. Don't get me wrong, there have been some days that I have cried to myself, but I know God. And, because I know God, my good days outweigh my bad days, so I have few complaints. When Bobby McFerrin came out with the song, *"Don't Worry, Be Happy"*, I made that my motto.

I have had health issues. There have been a couple of times when the doctors looked at my children and shook their heads, as if to say I wasn't going to make it. But, God said differently, and I am still here, laughing, and enjoying life.

When I was a little girl, I wondered some days if my mother loved me. She was a mean woman, who made my sister and I sleep outside at night, in the cold air, while she and her husband slept in the warm house.

It used to bother me that my mother could treat her children so cruelly. But I learned something from that experience. I learned, that because I was mistreated as a child, not to mistreat other people's children, especially my own. I learned that all children deserve to be loved, and I have been determined to show my own children love everyday.

When I began teaching, I was able to pick up on the signs of children who needed some extra love and attention. I was determined to be a teacher who showed compassion and understanding towards her students. I enjoyed my job, and was doing it because it rewarded me from a personal standpoint to be able to help children in a positive way. I didn't become a teacher for the money, because as it has been pointed out time and time again that teachers don't make that much money.

As a parent, I have been determined to show my children that I loved them everyday. Since I didn't believe that I was loved as a child, I want my children to never have to doubt that I love them.

I have been a supportive mother, who taught my children from an early age to love the Lord. I may not be the perfect mother in some people's opinion, but my children love and respect me, and that's what matters.

My children are successful, productive, Christian women, who went to college and made positive choices in life.

I am a giving and caring person. I will give my last to help somebody, especially children. I know what it's like to go without, or to want something so bad, and not be able to have it. I know what it's like not to have a new pair of shoes, or a new dress. I know what it's like to be picked on by the other children, and be called mean and hurtful names.

I could dwell on the fact that I was mistreated by my mother, but what good would it do?

I could wallow in self-pity and make excuses for not being a good mother, but how would that benefit me or my children?

I could have mentally abused my children and made them go without, and use the excuse that it's what I was taught as a child, but what purpose would it serve?

I could hate my mother, but then I wouldn't be living the way God teaches us to live in His Word.

I am a happy, single, Christian mother and grandmother, who finds laughter in every day, and who is determined to love and pray for others, especially those who don't love themselves. Life is too short to be sad. I encourage others to find some enjoyment in life. God gave us too many special moments in life for us not to be able to find happiness in one of them.

I know it's easier said, than done, but *don't worry, be happy!*

THE WAY I WALKED

God has been truly good to me. I have been blessed to live nine decades. I was a little girl during the Great Depression of 1929, and a grown woman when World War II began. I was a teenager in 1936, when Jesse Owens, a black athlete, competed for the United States in the track and field competition of the Berlin Olympics, and won four gold medals. My children were grown when President John F. Kennedy was assassinated in Dallas, November of 1963. I am grateful to that young preacher, Dr. Martin L. King, Jr. for all his hard work during the Civil Rights Movement, and I was deeply saddened by his death in April of 1968. I have been around for seventeen United States presidents. I must say, I was so proud to be here to see our first black president, Barak Obama elected.

I love to cook, especially baking pies and cakes.

My favorite book is the Bible.

My husband and I have been married for seventy-years. I was eighteen, and have been deeply in love with the handsome young man God sent to me every since we have been married. We met at church. When he tells the story to our children, he says that it was the way I walked that made him notice me. I laugh when I think about it because I just, walked. No special way, not sultry way, I just put one foot in front of the other, and walked. When he tells his side of the story to our children, he says that he knew the first time he laid eyes on me, that I was going to be his wife.

He was persistent, I must say, and was so kind and cute. I have to admit that I fell in love with him. We dated for a few months, and then he asked me to marry him. After a year of dating, and with our parent's permission, we married.

I was determined to be a good wife.

After awhile, my husband decided that it was time for us to have children. So, we did. Every two years, until we had eight of them. I have seen all my children grow up, and they are all still living. Each one different. Each one with a distinguished personality. They all think that I have a favorite. Honestly, I love them each the same, because they are all my babies. I carried each one close to my heart. I disciplined them all, loved them all, nurtured them all, cooked and cleaned up after them, with help from my husband, who never made me think that I was beneath him or less valuable than him because he was the man, the head of the household, and I was the wife. He loved me, and although we may have had disagreements from time to time, we made it. We built a home, we didn't just have a house.

We brought our children up in the church, and we brought the church into our home. My husband was a deacon, and I was a deaconess. We both worked, and taught our children the value of hard work, and the importance of a good education.

I have no major complaints. I was taught at a young age that God is the head of our lives, and that we should seek him daily for guidance and direction. Praying, and studying the Word have been a daily part of my routine for as long as I can remember. I have always been determined to be a good person, the kind that God would be pleased with.

I won't say that I haven't cried over some of the things in my life that have disappointed me, but I have made it my point to wear a smile on my face, to have a loving heart, and I make it a point to speak kind words to others. I have no need to be negative, and I purpose in my heart to love everybody.

Every day is a blessed day. Especially, when you wake up able to see, hear, walk, breath on your own, have reasonably good health and think, in your right mind. But if God happens to take just a piece of your good health, remember that it's only a test of your faith.

My strong, caring and productive mate for life is confused at times. The doctor calls it dementia. Some days, he doesn't remember everything, but when given a little time, certain memories came back to him. One memory he always seems to have is of how the two of us met.

Not too long ago, I found out that I had cancer. Most people give up, but I, with the love and support of my children, and grandchildren, fought cancer. Some days were hard, but I kept a positive attitude, and I beat it.

41

Whenever it seemed like my children and grandchildren were worrying more than I was, I would just smile and say, "It's alright Honey. Everything will be alright."

I know that I am blessed and highly favored.

I am thankful for every new day I experience.

God has smiled on me and my family, and I am determined, as I live to see another decade come to pass, to be thankful for His many blessings.

THE ALABASTER BOX

Matthew 26:7-13;7)There came unto him a woman having an alabaster box of very precious ointment, and poured it on his head, as he sat at meat. 8)But when his disciples saw it, they had indignation, saying, To what purpose is this waste? 9)For this ointment might have been sold for much, and given to the poor. 10)When Jesus understood it, he said unto them, Why trouble ye the woman? for she hath wrought a good work upon me. 11)For ye have the poor always with you; but me ye have not always. 12)For in that she hath poured this ointment on my body, she did it for my burial. 13)Verily I say unto you, Where so ever this gospel shall be preached in the whole world, there shall also this, that this woman hath done, be told for a memorial of her.

When I was a little girl, this scripture didn't mean very much to me. It was a scripture that I heard my mother and the Sunday School teacher read. Yet, like so many other scriptures I heard, I knew that the most important part of the scripture was that it mentioned Jesus.

Our family was taught at an early age how important God was, and the Bible was a significant symbol in our home. I remember seeing my mother read the Bible in her quiet time, and she reminded us to pray to God each day, because she was praying for us.

As a child, we pray because it is what we are taught to do. Most of us learn the child's prayer:

"Now I lay me down to sleep,
I pray the Lord my soul to keep.
Thy love guard me through the night,
and wake me with the morning Lord."

Or,

"Now I lay me down to sleep,
I pray the Lord my soul to keep.
If I should die before I wake,
I pray the Lord my soul to take."

My siblings and I were raised in a somewhat strict environment. The girls weren't allowed to date until they were sixteen, and sometimes, depending on who the date was with, the date still didn't happen. The closeness of family was stressed to us, as was the importance of sharing. Our dad was a doctor, so the importance of a college education was impressed upon us daily. We had to make good grades in school, and our dad's ultimate dream was for all of his children to become doctors, too.

That sounded great growing up. Yet, as we got older, and began making our own career choices, that wasn't something we all wanted to do.

Although I didn't want to be a doctor, I stayed close to our dad's dream, by studying Nursing.

While in college, I studied hard. I was smart, and I loved math. I devoted most of my time to studying, but tried to have some balance with fun and work. Of course, I became more knowledgeable about God, as I studied His word for myself, and was able to understand what those scriptures I heard as a child really meant. I developed my own relationship with God, one created out of understanding and much studying. My prayer routine changed drastically from that I had as a child. I learned the importance of praying not just at night before I went to bed, but throughout the day. I prayed before I did homework, I prayed before I took exams, I prayed for others, and with others, but mostly I prayed for myself, that I would be the woman that God created me to be.

Of course, just like in the movies, I met a young man, and fell in love. He was so cute! And a young minister, of all things.

He made me laugh. He was kind and compassionate. He was sensitive to my needs, and supportive of my educational pursuit. He had manners too. He opened doors for me, pulled out my chair when I would sit at a table, and even offered to put his jacket over a water puddle one time, so that my feet wouldn't get wet.

Although he attended college several hundred miles away, we maintained a long distance relationship. We spent countless hours on the phone, and never grew tired of the sacrifices we had to make, in order for our growing relationship to continue to grow. Neither of us had much money, so we put a lot of thought into tokens of love we gave each other on special occasions such as anniversaries, birthdays and Christmas. Anniversaries? You know, the anniversary of our first date, the anniversary of when we first met. Of course, those memories are important to a young couple.

I was determined to let this man that I had grown to love, who was a man of God, who showed his love for me, and respected me, know that I was committed to making our relationship work.

I had seen many young couples go through so much drama with dating. Breaking up with each other, then having to start over with someone else. Breaking up again, and again. The whole process was so dramatic. I witnessed friends crying, and going days without eating or sleeping. I witnessed friends missing classes, and sitting in their rooms, in a daze listening to love songs by Mary J. Blige and Keith Sweat. I saw sadness in their eyes, and empathized with them because I too, had experienced some of this magnitude of sadness when I was in high school and broke up with a boyfriend my senior year.

My own parents didn't have the most perfect marriage. Although my parents loved each other, they had their good days and bad days as well. It was during those bad days, that I would see my mom go into her secret closet and study God's Word. I would see her cry, and hear her whispered prayers. It hurt my heart to see her struggling to maintain her vows she made before God. Somehow, she managed.

After we dated for a year, we began talking about our future. *OUR* future, together. We were making plans about where we would live, and what kind of home we would own. We didn't want children right away, because we wanted to have time to get to know each other. We briefly discussed people who would be in our wedding, and talked about places to go for our honeymoon.

We talked about so many things. So, I knew that eventually, my Prince Charming was going to officially ask me to marry him. I was so excited, and every time I saw him, I anticipated that it would happen. Sometimes, as I think back, I got discouraged after a date where he didn't ask. It was

45

so frustrating because I knew it was coming, but it seemed to be taking so long. I knew that I had to stay focused on school, and graduating, but I loved him so much and was ready to start my chapter of life as a wife. I could still finish school, and be a wife. I had worked it out in my head. I could do this. I was ready, and determined that things were going to work, and I would be able to have my own *Happily Ever After* fairytale.

One evening, when I had managed to put the anticipation of a marriage proposal out of my mind, my Prince took me out to dinner. Not just any dinner. This was a special dinner. So special, he had reserved a special room at the restaurant where we could have some privacy. The table was set up so beautifully, and for some reason, when he pulled my chair out for me to sit down, the rest of the world seemed to disappear. As he set down across the table from me, and I looked into his eyes, it dawned on me, that there was something different about him that night. His eyes, and the look on his face was so serious.

We talked for a few minutes, and before our food arrived, my Prince took a box from his pocket. It was a special box. No, it wasn't a ring box. It was a different kind of box. *An Alabaster Box.*

As I looked at him, wondering what to think, he got up from his seat, walked over to me, kneeled down on one knee, and took my foot from underneath the table. He removed my shoes. He then opened the alabaster box, and took out a small bottle of oil, blessed oil, and began to anoint my feet one at a time. Tears came to my eyes.

Historically, alabaster was a symbol of purity and great honor. Alabaster was very expensive in Bible times, and if a person bought an Alabaster box, it was only used for very important purposes. So the Pharisees considered it a waste when a woman poured perfume from an Alabaster box on Jesus' head in Matthew 26:7-9. But the woman did not just wash Christ, but ANOINTED him! And my future husband was anointing me, his future wife.

Then, it finally happened, he pulled out another box! This one had a ring in it, and my Prince asked me to marry him.

The significance of the ring for me will always be important.
However, the loving gesture my husband expressed that night as he anointed my feet from the oil of the Alabaster box was so symbolic. He not only anointed me to be his wife, he knew that God's anointing would be on our marriage, and that for better or for worse, for richer or for poorer, in sickness and in health, to love, honor and cherish, forsaking all others,

to have and to hold from our wedding day, forward, that we would have God's blessing and favor on our union as One.

After we were married, I continued school, and am now a nurse.

I am so thankful that God chose this Prince Charming for me, and every time I hear the scripture of the woman with the Alabaster box, I will think of the special night my Prince asked me to marry him.

The Alabaster box sits on a shelf in our home, and will forever be a reminder to us that our marriage is a symbol of purity and honor.

My husband and I are determined to stay true to our vows. We pray our separate prayers several times a day, but we also pray together, because the Bible teaches that wherever two or more are gathered in His name, that He will be in the midst. It is our desire that God is always in the midst of our lives.

BEANS AND CORNBREAD

I get up each morning wondering what God has in store for me.

What will she be like today? Will she recognize me as her husband? Will she be quiet, and reluctant? Will she be talkative and agitated? Will she remember me as the man she dated when she was sixteen or will she think I am just some stranger and feel frightened and alone?

Most nights, things are quiet. Some nights, there is a lot of excitement. When she searches for something she has misplaced, and can't find it, she gets upset. When she wants something, and can't find the words to tell me what it is, she becomes frustrated.

I love her just as much today as I did the day I married her. And even though she doesn't know my name now, when I look into her face, I can see her mind, trying to recall who I am.

We married young. Raised children, bought a home, took vacations, worked diligently in the church. We provided dinner for the Pastor and his wife on Sundays at least once a month.

She sang in the choir, served on the Mission board, served as a deaconess and the church clerk. I serve as a deacon.

We raised our children to believe in God, serve God and trust God. We taught them to pray and be thankful for the blessings God granted them.

When I think of my wife and the relationship she established with God, the Proverbs 31 woman comes to mind.

My wife was valuable to me and my family, more valuable than precious jewels. And, just like precious jewels, my wife sparkled daily in the way she carried herself.

I trusted her with the affairs of our home, our finances and our children. She took care of things, and I had no reason to doubt any decisions that she made, because she had our families best interest at heart.

All wives fuss about something, and mine was no different. She loved a clean, neat home, and she took pride in making our home something we were proud to call home. Even if she fussed sometimes, her main focus was in reference to something positive, never negatives.

She worked with her hands, sewing, mending, baking, gardening, ironing and cleaning.

One of the things I loved about my wife was her cooking. She had a way with food that made me look forward to every meal. I looked forward to the smell of eggs, rice, bacon and toast for breakfast. I loved the way she fixed red beans and cornbread. There was always a delicious made-from-scratch-cake or pie, homemade candy and cookies in the house. She even learned how to decorate cakes, and it was so amazing to watch her transform an ordinary cake into a masterpiece. I never had to worry about not having a hot, home cooked meal, because my wife handled the grocery shopping, although she would send me to the store from time to time to pick up something she had forgotten.

On Sunday mornings, she would wake up early, while the rest of the family was still sleeping and begin preparing Sunday dinner. Somehow, she managed to fix Sunday dinner and breakfast at the same time. She was some special cook, because she managed to do so much before Sunday School, and magically had dinner ready shortly after we walked through the door following morning services.

She planted a garden so that we could have fresh vegetables. Greens were another food that she cooked. They were so good, people would call her and ask her to fix some for them when they knew they were coming for a visit. She didn't mind, she loved cooking, and she loved the fact that those greens came from her garden.

Whatever my wife did, she put her heart into it. Whether decorating the house for Christmas, or planning for her Secret Pal parties, or preparing amazing dishes in large quantities for family reunions or the kids functions at school. She loved making arts and crafts, and worked with the youth at church during special occasions to make special projects. The youth looked forward to it, and she had just as much fun preparing for the project as the youth did doing it.

Sometimes at night, she would go over the checkbook to make sure that things were in order. She would stay up late at times planning and organizing the money that the bank said we had to make sure ends met from pay day to pay day.

My wife was a giving person. She worked at a place that allowed her to help people in need. If she knew that a child was in need of something, she made sure they got it. If she knew that a family was in need of something, she figured out a way for them to get it. She would prepare hot meals and take them to sick people. As a Missionary at the church, the group of women she worked with put together baskets at Thanksgiving and Christmas and gave them to families in need.

She always made sure that our family was appropriately dressed. We were a good looking family, and it was because of my wife's ability to dress us. She loved to shop, so whatever our family needed, no matter what the season, we had it, and she always got it on sale. We even looked good in our coats and gloves in winter. She took care of all of our needs. And while she was taking care of our needs, she had a nice collection of shoes and dresses and matching accessories in several closets throughout the house. I didn't mind. Because she was my wife, and if she looked good, then I looked good. We were a reflection of each other.

She was a strong woman who was well respected by everyone. She was also a woman who knew God and found happiness in serving Him, and always gave thanks to Him for the blessings He gave to our family. She was determined to do things that would be pleasing to God.

My wife spoke kind words to people. She was a good listener, and gave helpful, Christian guided advice. Our children could talk to her about anything. Many people found her to be a confident because of the way she respected them. She may not have agreed with every thing others said or did, but she didn't degrade them or put them down. She said what needed to be said, lovingly, and let them make their own decisions, good or bad.

She was always busy doing something, or thinking something, or planning something, or studying something. From sun up, to sun down, my wife was busy. Even if she sat in her favorite chair, she had clothes in her lap, folding them, or papers in her hand, reading over them. She was definitely able to multitask.

Our children respect and love her. They always planned special surprises for her. I'm sure they didn't always agree with every decision or rule she made, but as they got older, they realized that the things she made them do, or how she made them act, or the values she instilled in them, were for their own good. Our grandchildren, and great-grandchildren are crazy about their grandmother. Of course, she spoiled them every chance she got.

I love my wife. I love everything about her, from the way she wears her hair, to the shape of her body, to the gleam in her eyes, to the way she laughs, to the way she holds my hand when we are in public, to the way she used to fuss about little things, and later laugh at the fact that she had fussed about it in the first place.

She is the woman that God chose for me to spend my life with. She is the woman God handpicked for me. We have been through a lot over the years, and I can not imagine what my life would have been like if I had gone through it without her by my side, loving me, caring for me, encouraging me, praying for me. I can not imagine what life would have been like if she wasn't my help-meet.

So, when I recall the vows I made so, so many years ago, in the presence of God, our parents, family and friends, I meant them all. For better, or for worse, in sickness, yes, in sickness, and in health. Even if she doesn't recognize who I am, I still recognize that she is my love, my life, my joy, my wife. Although Alzheimer's has taken her thoughts and distorted the pictures she sees in her head, I love her still, and will care for her, and treat her with all the love and respect she deserves.

Sometimes, I hear her singing and it's like nothing has changed. Her voice comes through so clear and strong, hitting every note, pronouncing every word, appearing to feel the words in which she sings.

> "Amazing grace, how sweet the sound, that saved a wretch
> like me. I once was lost, but now I'm found. Was blind,
> but now I see-"

Every now and then, as I'm standing in the kitchen trying to decide what to prepare us for dinner, I see the pot that was used to prepare many meals of red beans. Then I see the skillet that was used to prepare many batches of hot water cornbread. Then, I look at my beautiful wife, and remember the good old days.

As I smile to myself, I know that God allowed her to care for me and my children all of those years. So, I have no qualms about taking care of her now. I am determined to do whatever it takes to make her comfortable, keep her safe and shower all the love I have in my heart upon her.

NOTHING LIKE THE COSBY SHOW

I lie awake at night. Sometimes, I see him. Sometimes, I feel him. Sometimes, I smell him. Sometimes, I hear him. Sometimes, I cry for hours. Sometimes, I hate him. Sometimes, I miss him. Sometimes, I wish I could talk to him, and tell him how I feel.

Although it's been many years ago, the memories I have are so vivid, as if it just happened.

I was a teenager. A smart, cute girl who enjoyed reading, and being around my family. I was quiet, well mannered, but above all, I was a good student. My family attended church regularly.

I had lots of uncles, and aunts. Just like most kids, I had a favorite aunt. One that always made me feel warm and welcome when I visited her home.

My grandfather was one of my favorite people. He was so cool, and down to earth. He treated his grandkids, especially me, like we were special.

My grandmother was an amazing woman. She raised a large family, which I guess was the norm for most families during that time. I couldn't imagine having that many children. But, God knows who is, and who isn't equipped to have that many children.

It was from my grandparents that I learned how important family is, and what family should be about. It was from them that I learned about honor, respect, loyalty and pride. I learned that family stuck together, no matter what. I learned that divorce was not an answer, and that the elders had so much to share, and pass along to the younger generation.

Like most families, my parents had problems. We were not like the

Cosby show, or the Walton's. There were arguments and moments of silence. But for the most part, everything was ok.

I loved hanging out with my dad. He was very supportive and attended my games at school. My mom taught me how to cook, and clean, and all the other important things a mother teaches her daughter.

He came into my room one night. At first, I didn't understand what was happening. Then it became clear. My father was touching me in a way that no father should think of touching his daughter. He was doing things to me that he should be doing with his wife. I froze. I didn't know what to do. I didn't know what to say.

It happened again. And again. And again. For years.

Yes, my mother was home.

Why didn't I tell her? Why didn't I tell somebody? I was afraid that no one would believe me. I felt that it was my fault that it happened. Like, I had done something to make him feel as though it was okay to do to me the things that he did.

When others were around, everything was normal. When we were alone, things were tense. I tried to be away from home as much as possible so that there wouldn't be an opportunity for it to happen.

I wondered what it would take for him to stop.

I wondered if I didn't allow him to do it to me, would he do it to my sister.

I wondered if he was doing it to my sister, too.

I wondered if he felt guilty.

I wondered what made him think it was okay.

I wondered if I was the only girl in the world who's father was having sex with her.

I wondered if my mother could hear what was going on in my room.

My mom started acting differently towards me. She talked to me differently. She looked at me differently.

I wondered if she knew what her husband, my father had been doing to me. I wondered if she had seen him coming from my room. I wondered if she had confronted him. I wondered if he denied that anything was going on. I wondered why she never asked me.

I wondered why she didn't notice the change in my personality.

I wondered why she didn't notice the sad look in my eyes.

I wondered why she didn't notice how he disappeared from her bed at night.

I wondered if she blamed me.

I wondered if she noticed a difference in his behavior.

I wondered if she noticed the way he looked at me.

I wondered if she felt guilty.

I wondered, why, if she suspected that something was going on, why she didn't do anything to protect me, her daughter.

I wondered if she was ashamed of him.

I wondered if she was ashamed of me.

I wondered if she was ashamed of herself for doing nothing to make it stop.

For so many years, I allowed what my father did to me to have a hold on me. I have gone through moments of depression. I have had suicidal thoughts. I have felt guilty because of the way my mother acts towards me, and I have felt unloved at times, wondering what I could do to change things.

No, my family life wasn't like the Cosby show. I don't recall any episodes where Cliff slipped into Rudy, Denise, or Vanessa's room at night, and had sex with them while Claire slept down the hall. I don't recall any episodes where Claire didn't show love towards her daughters, or sit down with them when they started acting differently. I recall lots of laughs, and unbelievable family moments that seemed scripted and unrealistic, although fairy tale oriented. I don't recall seeing an episode that didn't end with some member of the cast smiling and laughing as the end credits began to roll.

One thing that keeps me strong is God's Word. It was instilled in me at a young age. I read my Bible when I need strength and courage. When the nightmares come back to haunt me, I pray to God to take them away.

I went to counseling for awhile. It helped, some. I realized that it was not my fault, and that I needed to not blame myself for the actions of my father. I realized that I couldn't make my mother treat me differently, or show love towards me. It was something she would have to purpose in her heart to do.

My counselor suggested that I write my father a letter, to express my feelings for what he had done to me when I was younger. I thought about it, and I tried to figure out just what to say. A strange thing happened though, while I was trying to figure out how to deal with the thoughts, and nightmares and guilt that I had been carrying. God took them away from me.

Yes, I still think about it from time to time, but it doesn't weigh on my mind, or keep me up at night.

As a product of incest, I know the signs of an inappropriate look, or touch that is attached to an inappropriate relationship between a man and a child. I know the sad look in a young girl's eyes, or the flinch from a seemingly innocent touch that may go unnoticed or unrecognized by others.

I am determined, to pay attention to my own children, to my nieces and nephews, to my friend's children, to the children I see at church. I am determined to pick up on those warning signs, and be an advocate of protection and encouragement for those who cannot always protect themselves, and may need a little encouragement to realize that it isn't their fault if they are molested by a stranger, a family member or a family friend.

I am determined to not let negative thoughts and repressed memories rule my life. I am determined to not let the uncaring and selfish actions of others take away my joy.

I am determined to be happy, to love myself, to love others, to forgive others, and accept the things that I cannot change, because I have the courage to change the things that I can, and I have the wisdom to know the difference. I am determined to find the good in others, no matter how hard it may be at times. I am determined not to let what my father did to ruin the faith and trust I had in him, keep me from forgiving him and loving him.

Although my relationship with my mother may never be what my heart thinks it should be, I am determined to honor her. I will pray for her, and have faith that God will change her heart, because I am worthy and deserving of love and respect from others.

I am fearfully and wonderfully made, because God said so.

GRAND-MOM

As a grandmother, I was so excited when my son told me he and his wife were going to have twins. What grandmother wouldn't be? Grandchildren are such a blessing, and the news of twins just creates more excitement. Two babies, at one time. I would get to spoil them, and love them, baby-sit from time to time and max out my credit cards at Christmas.

My son was a great father. He loved the boys and spoiled them. Wherever he went, there were two little heads tagging along. One with blonde hair, the other with brown. One, the image of my son, the other, the image of their mother. It was unbelievable how each parent had a small mirror image of themselves. As the boys began to develop personalities, it was clear that the parent the twin looked like, was the parent the twin acted like.

My son was mild mannered and happy, and caring. His wife wasn't. But, as the saying goes, opposites attract. Yet, as time passed, the two realized that their relationship wasn't working. So, my son agreed to keep the boys. He knew it would be hard raising them alone, but he also knew that his family would be there to help him. As his mother, I was determined to help him as much as I could.

As the boys started school, it was evident that one of the twins was having more trouble adjusting than the other. He would have more restroom accidents, and sometimes displayed a mean streak that would get him in trouble with his teachers. They were just three-years-old, but their personalities were very much developed.

Some days, it was a struggle with the boys. My son, tried as hard as he could to show patience and understanding with him. There were days when we would talk and he'd share with me how difficult it was at times, dealing with the twins different levels of behavior. One twin threw tantrums, and the other didn't. One was always smiling, while the other had to be coaxed to smile.

The summer came. And with it, the opportunity to enjoy the lake and all the wonders of nature that God created. My son decided to buy a boat. He thought it would be fun to take the twins fishing, and he always looked for ways to spend quality time with them.

One sunny day, my son took his new boat and the twins out on the lake. While on the lake, my son noticed that the boat was filling up with water. His first thought must have been of the twins, because when they were found floating in the water, wearing life jackets, they were clinging to each other. The older twin said that my son told him to take care of his brother as they watched him sink with the boat.

I was devastated. The local news stations kept replaying the story of my son's drowning and of the two little boys that had been found sunburned, holding onto each other as they waited for help.

For the twins sake, I could not wallow in my own pity. I had to be strong for them, as hard as it was. No mother wants to bury her child. My heart was aching.

I did the best I could with the twins after their dad died. Some days, I wondered what in the world was God doing when he made grandmothers become the mothers of their grandchildren. I loved my grandsons, and tried to do everything I could to make their lives happy and normal. My other son and daughter helped me.

I am getting older. A few more wrinkles and a lot more grey hair than when I first became grand-mom to the twins. I have had to deal with bad attitudes, arguments, brotherly fights, messy rooms, phone calls from school, and I have even found myself a little under the weather. My own mother needed me to care for her, as she had grown too ill to care for herself.

No matter how much extra stuff life seemed to add to my plate, I was determined that I wasn't going to let my son down. I was determined to see the twins grow up and be responsible, hard working men, just as their dad had been.

This year, the twins will graduate from high school. I am not sure what the future holds for them, but I am sure that their dad will be watching over them every step of the way.

The journey of raising two boys to manhood hasn't been an easy one, but the determination I had as a grandmother, combined with much prayer, made each day easier to manage.

SHOPAHOLIC

I love to shop. Clothing stores, furniture stores, discount stores, arts and crafts stores, antique stores, home improvement stores- any kind of store! I love to shop! I buy things I already have, things I don't need, things I think will make others envious of me and things that I know will make people turn their heads.

I have a wallet full of credit cards, debit cards, a check book and a little cash. I love to spend money.

I buy the best of everything, or the most expensive things in the cheap store to make myself feel good. I am a shopaholic. I have an addiction to shopping.

I dress myself up, to cover up my imperfections. I have a big, fancy house, a fancy car, and I have an important job, all to make me look good on the outside.

When I was a little girl, I didn't have much. My family was poor, and I was the product of many hateful and demeaning jokes as a child. I wasn't considered cute, I was too skinny, and I was poor. My self-esteem was low, and I hated the life I lived.

I was determined to grow up, and get everything I wanted, to replace the things I didn't have as a child. So, I shop; in person, on the internet, over the phone, in the window, whatever way possible.

I admit that no matter how much I buy, I always need more because I am never satisfied with what I have. I sometimes look in my closet, and see clothes I have never worn, shoes I have never worn, and items that I can't figure out where to place in my home. I see things I have purchased sometimes, and wonder what was I thinking when I bought it. Sometimes, after I decide to buy new things, to replace the things I bought last year,

I give stuff away to people in hopes it will make me look good in their eyes.

I must admit, I don't make donations to people, or give new things away just out of the kindness of my heart.

I am not a charitable person, and I do things strictly for show. I also like to point out faults in others. I pick up on the negatives, and love to put people on display, to make myself shine.

I know it sounds bad, but I went through a lot growing up. I faced a lot of ridicule and nasty stares. I hated who I was, and always wished to be more than I was, or someone else.

Although I know I have an addiction to shopping, I am determined to replace my sad childhood with tangible objects.

THE BLUE JEAN JACKET

I always thought that I would have a son. Someone to carry on my legacy, my name. My wife and I tried for years, but were unable to have children of our own.

We had built a new home, one that we helped design. We were so proud of our accomplishment. We both had good paying jobs and we enjoyed hanging out with our friends. But, something seemed to be missing. We had a big house, but needed to add something special to it.

After much discussion, my wife and I decided that since we couldn't have a child of our own, we would adopt one. My wife contacted an agency, and the search began.

For months, the caseworker called us, showed us photos of children for us to pick from. I wasn't impressed by what I was seeing. I know it sounds like I was buying a car, but I wanted a child that blended in with our family. I wanted a child that looked like he or she could have been a product of my wife and I. Sounds crazy, but, being a man, it was something that was important to me.

My wife got discouraged. She thought that I was being uncooperative. I tried to convince her to just be patient because I knew what I was looking for. I was determined to not rush into making a choice because this was a lifetime decision.

One day, my wife got a phone call while she was at work. The caseworker said that she believed she had found the perfect child for us.

As we drove to the adoption agency, my wife was nervous. Nervous because she felt that I was going to have a problem with this child, like I had with the others we had seen before. I was hoping that the trip wouldn't be a waste of our time. I was tired of going back and forth, looking at children. I felt bad that I had to say no to a child who needed to be loved, who needed and deserved parents.

As we walked into the building, I noticed this beautiful little girl in a room. She was about two-years-old. She was trying desperately to put on a blue jean jacket that was inside out. She was determined, and the longer we watched her, the more I fell in love with her.

When the caseworker entered the room, I looked her in the eyes and told her that I wanted the little girl in the room who was trying to put on the blue jean jacket. My wife looked surprised that I was finally making a decision.

We were allowed to take the little girl home with us that day. She was so beautiful even with the tears that fell from her eyes.

She cried for thirty minutes after we left the adoption agency. My wife tried to calm her down, but she only stopped crying when she fell asleep.

It only took a few weeks for our new daughter to get used to us. Our family and friends were happy that we had a new addition to our family. Many commented that our new daughter looked like she could be our real daughter. My wife would softly reply that she was our real daughter. From then on, the subject of adoption was not brought up.

As luck would have it, a family member's child had overheard the talk about the new addition to our family. When she asked her mother what adoption meant, her mother explained to her that children whose parent's didn't want them, were taken to a place where other people could adopt them.

When my daughter was six-years-old, she asked my wife if she was adopted. Surprised that our daughter had brought the subject up, we asked her who had told her she was adopted. She told us about the conversation she had with a cousin.

We were so upset that a child had told our daughter something that was private, and personal. It was a subject that we, her parents, should have had the opportunity to discuss with her.

My wife and I had already prepared ourselves for the day that would come when our daughter would find out that she was adopted. We had decided to just be honest with her, and tell her that she was adopted, and that because she was adopted, she was special. We told her the thing that made her special was the fact that we chose her out of all the other children we met to love.

That little girl, who captured my heart while trying to put on the blue jean jacket, loved to dance with me. I loved to hear her laugh, and made sure that she knew she was beautiful. She was truly special to us.

As parents, of a little girl who was adopted, we were determined to never make her feel adopted. We always treated her the only way we knew how; we loved her, and that was what she needed for us to do.

I recall her first Christmas with us. My wife and I went crazy making sure that Santa Claus left the right toys for our little girl. Our living room looked like a toy store on Christmas morning. Our little girl's eyes were so big as she went from toy to toy. Being a kid at heart, I was smiling just as hard as she was. I felt like a kid in a toy store too, as I played with her that Christmas morning.

I went to school plays and programs. Whatever she was in, I was there. I enjoyed watching her dance around on stage like a little ballerina.

She hardly got in trouble, but when she did, I left the discipline to my wife. I believe I only spanked her twice in her life, and I am sure that it didn't hurt her. It probably hurt me more, because I avoided punishing her.

When she was in the seventh grade, she started experimenting with makeup. She said the rest of the kids were doing it.

All I could think of was how naturally beautiful she was, and I told her that because she was naturally beautiful, she didn't need to wear makeup. What I said must have meant a lot to her, because I don't recall seeing her wear makeup after that.

I remember when the boys started paying attention to her. *A father's nightmare.* I knew that the time would come, but I don't think I was truly prepared for it. I had a rule. No dating until she was sixteen.

I remember one night, I think she was thirteen, a boy called the house and asked to speak to my daughter. I told him that my daughter was not allowed to talk on the phone to boys, and that she couldn't date until she was sixteen. He was very polite, and said that he would call back then. Amazingly, he did just that. My daughter was so surprised when he called her three years later. She had forgotten all about him, but for some reason, he hadn't forgotten about her. Needless to say, she had no interest in him, and he didn't call but a few times.

One day, when our daughter was fourteen, her mother and I got into an argument. I don't remember what it was about, because we argued often. I said some stupid things, and one of them was that we should have left our daughter at the orphanage. I think I was jealous of the amount of time and attention my wife spent with her. I didn't realize that our daughter heard me, but I noticed how quiet she had been and how standoffish she was with me. I found out from my wife that she had overheard the comment I'd made about the orphanage.

I felt so bad. My wife had tried to reassure her that I hadn't meant anything by what I said. But, I could tell that my little girl's feelings were hurt. I, had to man up. I had to apologize to her, and let her know that what I said was done so in the heat of the moment, and that I loved her. I tried to remind her of what we had always taught her, that she was special because we got to choose her. It took a while for her to forgive me.

My daughter grew up to be a beautiful young woman. She went to college, got married, and had children. Every time I see her, I think back to that first day I laid eyes on her. That beautiful little girl, who was determined to put on that blue jean jacket, no matter how long it took. Amazingly, she is still just as determined today, as she was then.

And, I, have been determined to assure her that I didn't mean the inconsiderate statement I made, by showing her how much I love her, and appreciated her being my only daughter.

TORNADO SEASON

As I lay there, crumpled on the floor like a rag doll, the taste of warm blood dripping from my lips, my right eye blurred and my head pounding, I asked God to help me. Part of me wanted to just lie there and give up, and not fight back. After a few seconds, I could feel anger rising up inside of me as my heart raced, and I recall my fists forming a ball.

As tears began to form in my eyes, I guess it was my guardian angel that picked me up off the floor and planted me steadily on my feet. At that moment, I decided I was ready to fight for my life!

"Chris", the man that I thought loved me, had made a big mistake. He had mistaken my kindness for weakness, and my trust for stupidity. Somewhere in his mind, he had the idea that I was weak, and afraid. He thought that I wouldn't fight back.

He was wrong!

A few years before I met "Chris," I dated a guy who was perfect, in the beginning. We had a lot in common. He was cute, of course, and he thought that I was beautiful. I guess that's something every woman wants to hear from her man. He loved my cooking. We both loved football, the Dallas Cowboys of course! We both liked to party, and drink occasionally. He was easy to talk to and we spent a lot of time together.

One day, we got into an argument over something so trivial, I don't even recall what it was. He got in my face, there was screaming and shouting. One thing lead to another, furniture had been knocked over, and we both had scratches and bruises. There were traces of blood on the floor by the time the police showed up to my apartment. I had never experienced a man hitting me, and I told myself that that was something

I would never experience again. The way it made my heart feel, crushed and broken. The way it made me doubt my ability to choose a decent mate. The way it made me not trust other men afterwards. I was deeply affected by the incident.

I remember the day "Chris" and I met. I thought he was so fine. He was a little older than me and he had children. With the children came baby mama drama, of course. He had a job, a nice car and he always had money. Above all, he respected me and that was important.

After we dated for a short while, he introduced me to his children, who seemed to really like me. They were cool, they were respectful, and eventually I began spoiling them, by buying them toys and clothes and whatever they asked for whenever they came over.

His mom and sisters treated me like family.

My mom was kind of hard to read, and I couldn't really tell if she liked him or not. She was cordial to him, and said as long as I was happy, she was happy for me.

After we dated for awhile, "Chris" and I moved in together. Things seemed fine at first, but then things began to change.

I've often heard people say you don't truly know someone until you live with them, and that was definitely true for "Chris". He became irritable at times, and I came to see a side of him that I didn't know existed. My perfect man, the one I was in love with, was a drug dealer. How I didn't see it before, I have no idea.

Somewhere along the way, I got mixed up. I started sampling some things I shouldn't have, and I lost myself.

"Chris" and I began to fight often. He was bigger than me, so my petite frame was no match for him. But I fought back anyway!

One thing I learned the hard way, after being with "Chris" was that drugs, alcohol and hot tempers don't mix. We would fight, and break up. We would make up, and for a while things would be cool.

I lost my job, and he told me he would take care of me. And, he did. But it wasn't long before we were fighting again.

One day, the thought came to me that I needed to stop putting drugs into my system so that I could focus on my life and my jacked up relationship with "Chris". I became depressed. I couldn't believe that I had allowed myself to get to the sad place that had become my life.

I even believed that "Chris" was cheating on me with the mother of his children. That was messed up.

One day, while sitting alone in that apartment, listening to Mary J. Blige, drinking a beer and smoking a cigarette, I thought about all the mess I had been going through with "Chris". I realized that I didn't love him. As tears began to stream down my face, I started to realize that I hated him for the way he made me feel. I hated myself for falling for his good looks, his charm, his lies. I hated myself for allowing him to talk to me any kind of way, to say hurtful things and profane words to me. I hated myself for needing him. I hated myself for getting caught up in this drama that had become my life.

My phone rang. It was my best friend, Big Red. We met in high school. She was high yellow, as we mocha shaded people say about light skinned people. So, the name "Big Red" just seemed appropriate.

She had no idea what I was going through, but throughout the years, whenever one of us was going through a really hard time, the other seemed to call at just the right time. It was like God had given us the vision to be able to sense trouble in each other's lives.

That day, she could tell that something wasn't right, and asked just enough questions to find out everything, even though I gave no real answers. I hated the way she could do that. She was like a mind reader.

That day, she told me some things that I needed to hear. She told me that I was too good to be in the situation that I was in. She told me that I was too beautiful to waste my life with "Chris". She said I deserved better than to allow him to physically and emotionally abuse me. She said that I had to want things to be different and they would be. She reminded me that I didn't have any children with "Chris" and that it would be easy for me to cut ties with him.

We didn't talk long. But by the end of the conversation, I felt much better, and stronger about what I needed to do.

A few days later, after I had gathered my former, pre-Chris-pre-drama-pre-love-confused-with-need, pre-alcoholic, pre-drug-sampling, pre-emotionally-damaged, pre-loss-of-self-worth-being, "Chris" and I got into an argument.

I saw fire in his eyes. I saw the devil in his face. And before I knew it, I was on the floor. Everything in me was determined to return with fury that same unloving punch that I had received from this ungrateful individual that I had cared for, whose children I had helped care for, and treated like my own, who I worried about, and gave a place in my heart to. This individual, whom I had lost my way because of. Who had the audacity to look at my beautiful face, and turn it into a punching bag, had no idea that it was about to become tornado season in the apartment that day!

After I had prayed to God to help me get up off the floor, I gathered myself together and I fought "Chris"! I forgot that I was that petite little thing that he hadn't imagined was full of fire!

I fought back, remembering every hurtful word spoken, every painful punch I had endured over the duration of our relationship. I recalled his encouragement of me beginning a habit that it took God's help for me to stop. I felt empowered! And, at some point, when he realized that I was fighting for my life, everything stopped. Time stood still, and he looked at me. I was poised for another round. He shook his head, wiped the blood from his lip, looked down at his ripped shirt, grabbed his keys off the floor, walked out the front door, and out of my life.

It took me a long time to trust again. I was satisfied just being by myself. Love and relationships seemed to be like tornados; unpredictable and destructive.

Yet, somewhere deep inside, I am determined that God didn't put me on this earth not to find true love, not to be loved, and not to show love. I am determined that the scars from my past relationships won't hinder what God has for me.

When I started repairing my heart, and my life, I began to love myself and see how beautiful I was. I realized that I was too beautiful to be miserable, too beautiful to be abused, too beautiful to destroy my body with drugs and too beautiful to be sad, depressed and stressed.

I am a beautiful woman, created by God, and I am determined to be happy, because God promised that the blessings of the Lord makes us rich and has no sorrow. Riches come in many forms, not just monetary. It is because of His promise, that I know when I am happy, and not stressed and sad, that God has blessed me with what is best for me.

AS LONG AS THE BILLS GET PAID

He may not be the best husband in the world, but at least the bills get paid.

He may cheat on me, with more than one woman at a time, but at least the bills get paid.

I have caught him, with other women, but at least the bills get paid.

I have had to fight other women over him, but at least the bills get paid.

He may hit me, kick me, leave bruises on my body, but at least the bills get paid.

He may stay out all night, and come home drunk, and high, but at least the bills get paid.

We may not have food to eat, because he spent it all gambling, and at the club, but at least the bills get paid.

I may be afraid to go to the doctor because I think I have a sexually transmitted disease, but at least the bills get paid.

My eye is black, and I can barely open it, but at least the bills get paid.

My right rib is broken and I can't move my left wrist, but at least the bills get paid.

I have bruises on my neck, because he tried to choke me, but at least the bills get paid.

He has threatened to kill me, because I asked him a question, but at least the bills get paid.

I have seen him in public with his other woman, but at least the bills get paid.

We have children, and they hear us fighting, but at least the bills get paid.

I hear my children in the other room crying, while I'm trying to keep him from hitting me again, but at least the bills get paid.

I have a nice house, but it isn't a home, but at least the bills get paid.

I was at the hospital having a baby, while he was out with his friends, but at least the bills get paid.

He curses at me in front of his friends, but at least the bills get paid.

He takes the money that I save for my kids shoes, and uses it to buy himself a bag of weed, but at least the bills get paid.

He wrecked his car, and then took mine, and I can't go to work, but at least the bills get paid.

He doesn't appreciate the things that I do for him, but at least the bills get paid.

I don't love him, but at least the bills get paid.

We only talk to each other when we have to, but at least the bills get paid.

I know I can do better, but at least the bills get paid.

I am glad when he is gone, but at least the bills get paid.

I flinch when he touches me, but at least the bills get paid.

I can't stand the sound of his voice, but at least the bills get paid.

I dread going home because I know he will be there, but at least the bills get paid.

His girlfriend calls my phone and hangs up, several times a day, but at least the bills get paid.

He didn't even remember my birthday, but at least the bills get paid.

He never buys me or the kids anything for Christmas, but at least the bills get paid.

I get ready to go to church on Sunday, but he says I can't go, but at least the bills get paid.

My baby needs pampers and milk, but he just bought himself new Jordan's, but at least the bills get paid.

My daddy says I should leave him, because things are only going to get worse, but at least the bills get paid.

My mama says he's going to kill me one day, but at least the bills get paid.

I know he doesn't mean it when he says that he loves me, but at least the bills get paid.

We go days without speaking to each other, but at least the bills get paid.

He threw me against the wall, but at least the bills get paid.

He hit me while I was holding my baby, but at least the bills get paid.

He punched me while I was driving down the street, but at least the bills get paid.

The lights got cut off, but at least some of the bills get paid.

The car doesn't work, but at least the bills get paid.

He body slammed me, but at least the bills get paid.

He broke my nose, but at least some of the bills get paid.

He broke my jaw, but at least the bills are getting paid.

Child Protective Services took my children, but at least the bills get paid.

His friend tried to talk me into leaving, said my husband was no good, but at least the bills get paid.

He has another baby on the way, by another woman, but at least the bills get paid.

They repossessed my car today, but at least some of the bills get paid.

They put an eviction notice on my door today, but at least some of the bills get paid.

I can't walk, I think my hip was displaced when he stomped me last night, but at least the bills get paid.

He burned me with a cigarette, then said it was an accident, but at least the bills get paid.

He put a gun to my head, and threatened to blow my brains out, but at least the bills get paid.

The gas was turned off today, but at least some of the bills get paid.

My baby needs medicine, but he just bought a new jersey for himself, but at least the bills get paid.

The police came by looking for him, but at least the bills get paid.

He tried to run me over with the car, but at least the bills get paid.

He almost burned the house down, when he fell asleep with a cigarette in his hand, but at least the bills get paid.

His girlfriend tried to kill me, but at least the bills get paid.

He pawned my wedding ring, so the bills could get paid.

He looks at my daughter inappropriately, but at least the bills get paid.

He took a knife, and held it to my throat, but at least the bills get paid.

He makes me, be intimate, even if I don't want to, but at least the bills get paid.

Sometimes he leaves for days at a time, and hits me when I ask where he has been, but at least the bills get paid.

He hit's the kids, for no reason, but at least the bills get paid.

He needs anger management counseling, but at least the bills get paid.

He goes through my cell phone to see who I have been talking to, and accuses me of being unfaithful, when I haven't been, but at least the bills get paid.

He goes through my stuff at night while I'm asleep, and sits over me until I wake up. I think he is loosing his mind, but at least the bills get paid.

He says nasty things to me in front of the kids, but at least the bills get paid.

He tells me who I can and can't be friends with, because he is the man of the house and what he says goes, but at least the bills get paid.

He allows his kids from a previous relationship to disrespect me, but at least the bills get paid.

He allows his family to disrespect me, but at least the bills get paid.

He can't keep a steady job, but at least the bills get paid.

He thinks women should be seen and not heard, but at least the bills get paid.

My self-esteem is gone, but at least the bills get paid.

I dream of ways to end my life, but at least the bills get paid.

He shoved me down a flight of stairs, and said he didn't mean to shove me so hard, but at least the bills get paid.

He opened the car door, while the car was moving, and told me to get out, but at least the bills get paid.

My children, haven't eaten in days, but he just bought some weed, but at least the bills get paid.

The school called and said my son punched a little girl, and said he saw his dad do it to me, but at least the bills get paid.

He said I couldn't talk on the phone to my sister, because she's always trying to tell me that I can do better than him, but at least the bills get paid.

He pawned the television, so the bills could get paid.

He locked me in the closet, and wouldn't let me out, but at least the bills get paid.

I know this relationship is unhealthy for me, but at least the bills get paid.

I can't sleep at night, because I am so depressed, but at least the bills get paid.

Sometimes, I wish he would die, and then, I would be free of him, and I know that's bad, but at least the bills get paid.

He calls me dumb and stupid, but at least the bills get paid.

He forgot our anniversary, and didn't even give me flowers on Valentines day, but at least the bills get paid.

He doesn't answer his cell phone when I call, although he carries it with him everywhere he goes, but at least the bills get paid.

I overheard him whispering on the phone, then he quickly hung up when I entered the room, but at least the bills get paid.

My hair is coming out, from all the stress from this relationship, but at least the bills get paid.

He calls me fat, but at least the bills get paid.

He lies to me all the time, but at least the bills get paid.

He busted my lip, but at least the bills get paid.

He said he was sorry, but I know he didn't mean it, but at least the bills get paid.

I don't want anyone else to have him, so I am determined to stay with him, because at least the bills get paid.

I am determined to be miserable, because as long as the bills get paid, it doesn't matter what he does.

SWEET TEA

She is so beautiful. So small. So fragile.

She is so innocent. So sweet. So amazing.

I can't believe that she is a product of me.

I had something to do with creating her. I can't believe that I am a dad. A dad. That means that someone will look up to me someday. That means that someone will depend on me someday. That means that I have been given the opportunity to love, protect, teach, comfort, nurture and cultivate this little princess that I held in the crevice of my arms.

So perfect. Her eyes, her lips, her nose, her hands, her feet. I know that I am going to have to be ready to stand my ground some day when this little princess wants to hear a yes, but needs to hear a no.

I wonder what she will be when she grows up. I wonder what her favorite color will be, and what her favorite food will be. I wonder if she will be a cheerleader, an athlete or a scholar. I wonder if she will be a class clown, like I was, or quiet and studious like my mother. I wonder if she will be tall, like her mother, or medium height. I wonder if she will have the gift of voice, like my brother, or photographic memory like me.

It's so scary. To think that someday, this precious little princess, will not have time for me, because she will be too busy with her friends, or talking on the phone, or listening to music, or living her own life. A life that hopefully I can help cultivate into something positive and beautiful.

I am young and have made so many mistakes in my life. But I'm trying to be the father that I need to be. I'm trying to become the man God created me to be.

Sometimes, when I have a lot on my mind, I go visit my mama. We sit in the kitchen, and I talk while she listens, and I drink some of her delicious sweet tea.

I love my mama's sweet tea. It's so addictive. Before I know it, I have had three or four tall glasses. I like fried okra and pizza too. But if I had to choose between quenching my thirst or stopping hunger pains, I will choose quenching my thirst with my mom's sweet tea.

She is a no nonsense type of woman. She is straight forward, and says what needs to be said, which isn't always what I want to hear. When my daughter was born, she had this talk with me about how important it was going to be for me to be a good father, to be a positive role model and to be there for her. She said that being a parent wasn't easy, and that I had to learn the difference in being a parent to my daughter, and not being her friend. She said that I was going to have to be mean to her sometimes, even if it hurt me because it would help her.

I remember hearing a lot of no's while growing up. I heard some yes's, but it seemed like the no's outweighed them. I remember asking for things that I didn't think were expensive, like hundred and twenty dollar Jordan's, or seventy-dollar jeans, or forty-dollar video games. It was funny because I got more no's from my mama, than my grandmother. I would get so upset sometimes that I couldn't get what I wanted. I vowed that when I had my own kids, I was going to buy them whatever they wanted, and I was going to let them do whatever they wanted, and I wasn't ever going to tell them no. I wasn't going to spank them, or fuss at them. I was going to let them stay up as late as they wanted, even if it was a school night. I wasn't going to make them have a curfew, and I wouldn't say anything about the people they hung out with. I wasn't going to say anything about their friends being rude when they called on the phone, and I definitely wasn't going to tell their friends that they couldn't receive phone calls after ten o'clock. They could drink up all the Kool-aid, because I could just make some more, and they wouldn't have to do any chores, because chores were dumb. They could eat up anything in the kitchen, and I would just buy some more. I would probably just buy paper plates and plastic cups and silverware so that they wouldn't have to wash dishes. There would be no such thing as a budget, because my kids wouldn't understand what a budget was anyway. If they didn't want to go to school everyday, it wouldn't matter if they didn't have a fever, or weren't throwing up, they could stay home sometimes, because I would understand that they were sick of school. I wouldn't fuss at them about cleaning up their room, because it was their room, and if they didn't want to pick their dirty clothes up off the floor, then they didn't have to. I wouldn't make them go to church if they didn't want to because church lasted too long, and it was a waste of a perfectly good day to sleep late. I wouldn't care what type of music they listened to, because it's just music, and I wouldn't care how much something cost, if they wanted it, I would get it for them.

I was determined to be a good father, no matter what.

My own father wasn't really there for me. He was in and out of my life. Growing up, I promised myself that I wouldn't be like him. I would be there for my children. I would be more than just a sperm donor.

There are some things about me that I need to change. I am not perfect. Sometimes I think that if it wasn't because I remember to pray everyday, I would be dead. I have been in so many situations that could have ended my life, but I know that because my mama prays for me, and because I pray for myself, I am protected by God's grace and mercy.

When my grandmother died, it broke my heart. My mama always tells me that my grandmother is my guardian angel, and that she watches over me. I believe that.

Sometimes, I think about what it is that I can do to be a better man. I tell myself that God has a plan and a purpose for my life. I grew up in church, so I know Bible stories and verses.

When I look at my daughter, I don't like to think about her growing up without me in her life. I want to be there for every tear that falls, every missing-toothed moment, every fashion change, every report card, every scrapped knee, every birthday and Christmas.

When I look at her as she grows each day, I am amazed at the cycle of life. I was so excited when she used to stare at me, and how she would turn her head when she heard my voice. I was excited when she began to roll herself over, and how she began to scoot from one end of the blanket to another in the span of a thirty minute television show. I remember when she started placing her hand underneath my armpits as I held her while she drank her bottle. It was so irritating, because it was like she was pinching me the whole time I was feeding her. I was delighted when she learned to say "*Daddy*", and when she started to crawl. It warmed my heart when she chose to come to me over her mother, or anyone else. When she started walking, it saddened me because my baby was growing up, and would soon be out of the stage of innocence.

One day, I was riding in the car with her. We were in the backseat. I was talking to my brother, and suddenly the car started to beep. My little princess had managed to reach the handle of the door, and made it open just enough to make the dinging noise begin. It scared me so bad, that all I could think to do was pop her hand. She cried. I felt so bad. She had big teardrops falling from her eyes. I moved as close to her as possible and tried to explain to my one-year-old that I would go crazy if something happened to her. I wiped the tears from her eyes, as they formed in my own. After she calmed down, I kissed her on the cheek, and held her hand. Thoughts went through my head. I had disciplined her! The same thing my mama and grandmother used to do to me. I had actually felt this feeling of authority come over me. I guess it was the thought of something happening to her that sent me into guardian mode. Whatever it was, I knew right then that all those things I said I wouldn't do, I would when it came to my daughter. I knew right then, that she would have to endure more no's than yes's from me, just as I did from my mama. I would care about the types of friends she had, and how she dressed. I would care about rude boys calling her on the phone, and she would definitely have a curfew. Her education would be important, and it would be important for her to keep her room clean and learn how to keep the house clean. No one likes a nasty person, especially a nasty woman. I realized that I wouldn't be able to buy her everything she asked for, although I would do my best to try and get her everything she needed and some of what she wanted. I knew that I would care about what she saw on television, and wanted her to only watch children's educational programs.

In that instant, I understood why my mama had been the way she was with me. It was because she loved me, and she didn't care about what other parents were doing for their children. She didn't care about what my friends didn't have to do, or how much their parents spent on their clothes and shoes. She didn't care that my friends didn't have curfews, or skipped school. She didn't care that their parents didn't know where they were, or didn't require them to check in every so often. She didn't care that I had an attitude or talked about not being able to wait until I was grown. She was my mama, and I was her child.

I remember one time I was so angry about something, I was talking under my breath, and my mama heard me. I know I was wrong, but I balled up my fists. Something in her eyes changed at that moment, and I saw her go from mama, to some type of beast. She backed me into a corner, and then I saw her go for the lamp that was on the table to her right. She didn't hit me with it, but she made me a promise that if I ever did hit her, I wouldn't hit anyone else. I'm still living, so enough said on that subject.

Boys2Men had this song called, "Mama's Song". It was from the *Soul Food* movie. That song means so much more to me now that I am a man, than it did when I was a child. The lyrics talk about appreciating everything that mama's do for their children, how they love and care for them, nurture them, teach them and guide them, encourage them and protect them. As a child, I didn't really care about that. I knew my mama said she loved me, and she would hug me and kiss me and tell me what she felt was right and wrong. When I became a man, when I became a father, I understood how important it was for me to appreciate every sacrifice my mama had made for me. I understood how sometimes when she wanted to say yes, she couldn't because money was tight. I understood that everything she taught me was for my own good, and that I would use so much of what she taught me, to teach my daughter.

When I listen to my daughter sing her *ABC's*, and count, and say with confidence that something red is purple, or when she brings me a book, then climbs into my lap, and looks up at me with those big, happy, brown eyes, waiting with anticipation, I think back to my mother reading to me, and taking every opportunity to teach me something.

It's funny how my little princess has her own little personality, a beautiful sweet smile, a distinguished angelic voice and a stubborn streak all rolled into one, tiny package.

Someday, I know that she will be sitting at my mama's table, an accomplished, beautiful young woman, sipping on a glass of sweet tea, talking about her thoughts and sharing her points of view.

I used to wonder why God chose my mama specifically for me. When I look at my daughter, and see my mama's genes on display like a painted portrait, I know that He gave me the mama that I needed. Not the one I wished I had. He equipped her with what she needed to build me up.

Every now and then, I call my mama just to hear her voice and tell her I love her, and appreciate her.

Sometimes, when I go to her house, and sit at the table, drinking a tall glass of sweet tea, I feel the need to tell her how sorry I am for some of the things I have done to disappoint her. I have even apologized for being disrespectful, and for not understanding why she had to be so stern with me at times. I admit to her that she was right, and I was wrong on a lot of situations. I tell her how one day, she is going to be really proud of me.

It doesn't matter that I am not perfect now, because I am determined that someday, I will be the man that God created me to be.

I am thankful that the woman who makes the best sweet tea in the world, my mama, prays for me, daily, even when I don't pray for myself.

1 Corinthians, 13:11: When I was a child, I spoke as a child, I understood as a child, I thought as a child, but when I became a man, I put away childish things.

TIRED

It was raining outside. I could hear the drops beating against the window. It was dark, and the sun hadn't come up yet.

As I rolled over in my bed, my cheek brushed against the tear stained pillow that cradled my head. I thought about getting up, but didn't have the *energy*.

I looked at the clock. It was five o'clock in the morning. I looked at the phone. I thought about calling a friend, but I knew it was too early. I turned over again. My mind was so busy. Too many thoughts crowding my mind.

I wanted to stop crying, but the gloominess of the weather didn't help uplift my spirit.

I thought about my childhood, and how happy I was growing up. I thought about friends, and memories of vacations I had taken. Those were good times.

What happened to those days? What happened to the good times? What happened to a good night's sleep? What happened to the days of smiling from ear to ear, and laughing until I cried?

Why had I allowed myself to get to this place? This place of sadness, depression and self-destruction? This place of sleeplessness, anxiety and loss of appetite.

I had been thinking about it for days. But, I couldn't make my mind up about how to do it.

I thought about taking pills, because they wouldn't be messy. I could just take them, and fall asleep, and never wake up.

I thought about running the tub full of water, and sliding slowly down into it, but couldn't decide if I would do it with my clothes on or off. I didn't want anyone to find me naked, and I wasn't sure about getting in a tub of water fully clothed. It just didn't seem natural.

I thought about cutting my wrists, but wasn't sure if I could go through with it. Then, I thought about the blood, and how messy it would be. I just wanted something simple.

I thought about using a gun, but since I didn't like them, I didn't think I would be able to pull the trigger.

I thought about getting in my car and driving into oncoming traffic, but didn't want to hurt anyone else in my desperate attempt to end my life.

I had talked to God. I had told Him I was tired of living. Tired of living in a world where it seemed like no one cared about me. Tired of living in a world where people only think of themselves, and what makes them happy. Tired of living in a world where people never give of themselves but expect you to give, give, give.

Tired of dealing with bills, and money issues. It just never seems to be enough of it. Tired of living check to check, and never having anything to show for it. Tired of taking care of one thing, and something else happening that requires me to come up with money I don't have.

Tired of dealing with unappreciative children who aren't the children I raised them to be. Tired of dealing with bad attitudes and disrespect when all I do is try to make life easy for them. Tired of dealing with teachers and bad grades, and arguing about what is and what isn't appropriate to wear. Tired of worrying about the friends they hang out with, and whether or not they will end up in juvenile, or jail. Tired of wondering why they are drinking since they are underage, and why they are using illegal substances.

Tired of dealing with an insignificant other who doesn't care, or show love in return. Tired of arguing, and feeling like I am unimportant and worthless. Tired of doing my part to make things work, when others don't do the same. Tired of being used and abused, misunderstood and lonely.

Tired. Just, tired.
No smile on my face.
Tired.
No feeling in my heart.
Tired.
Too tired to even think about a smile.
No joy.

Tired.
No happiness.
Tired.
Broken.
Tired.
Beaten.
Tired.
Confused.
Tired.
Alone.
Tired.
Heartbroken.
Tired.
Overworked.
Tired.
Unloved.
Tired.
Giving up.
Tired.
Giving in.
Tired.
All cried out.
Tired.
All argued out.
Tired.
Imperfect world.
Tired.
Rude people.
Tired.
Liars.
Tired.
Just end it all.
Tired.
Disappointed.
Tired.
Misunderstood.
Tired.
Just find a way to do it.
Tired.

Tired. Just tired.
Tired of living.

The sun came up. The rain had stopped. It was still cloudy.

As I sat up, and looked around my room, I saw something familiar that I had not touched in a while. It was my Bible.

I looked away from it, because God didn't seem to care about me.

If He cared about me, my life would be different.

If He cared about me, my children would be perfect.

If He cared about me, my relationship would be a loving one.

If He cared about me, I wouldn't have money problems.

If He cared about me, I wouldn't have so many issues.

If He cared about me, I wouldn't be so sad.

If He cared about me, I wouldn't feel lonely.

If He cared about me, I wouldn't be in so much pain.

If He cared about me, I would have someone to love me.

If He cared about me, I WOULDN'T BE FEELING LIKE THIS!!!

I lay back down on my bed, looking up at the ceiling. I thought back to a time when I used to love myself, when I wouldn't allow situations and circumstances to get me down. I thought back to how determined I used to be to make myself happy. I thought back to how God was the center of my joy and the head of my life. I thought back to how everything just seemed to work better when I had a relationship with God.

I pulled myself off the bed.

I looked up then got down on my knees.

I cried as I talked to God, and told Him all about my troubles.

I don't know how long I was there, on my knees, talking to Him, but slowly, my tears began to dry up. And my prayer that started out weak, became stronger. And my thoughts that were negative, became positive. And my despairing cry, turned into a powerful declaration of purpose. And my mind became clear. And my heart stopped aching. And my faith was restored.

I got up, off my knees, with a vision. A vision of which I was determined to not worry about anything. A vision of which I was determined to pray about everything. A vision of which I was determined to give it all to God, and take life the way we live, one day at a time.

I woke up that morning to storms, with my mind on dying.

I went to sleep that night, with peace, determined to live everyday, thankful to God for reminding me not to forget about Him.

I woke up tired.

I went to sleep rejuvenated.

BLACK AND BLUE

I remember lying on the floor. I think she body slammed me. I remember my head hitting the floor. It hurt so bad. Then, she was beating me, with her fists. I knew not to hit her back, so I just tried to shield her punches. It was like, she had gone crazy. I couldn't even see her face; all I could see were her fists. Then all of a sudden, she got up, and stood over me. She was so full of anger. She took her right foot, and stomped me in my neck.

I guess God had mercy on me, because she got tired, and told me to get out of her face. I could barely breathe, but I got up and limped away, body aching, battered and bloody in places. I wondered how many bruises she had left and I wondered how I would be able to cover them up.

The thought of calling the police or Child Protective Services never entered my mind. Back then, it was unheard of for a child to tell on a parent for beating them. I just took my beating that time, like I had done so many times before, and cried the pain away. Normally, I went to the bathroom afterwards, so that I could lock myself in, and assess the damage as I cried to myself.

My chest was black and blue. My arms had bruises all over them. This was definitely going to be a long-sleeved shirt week. My neck was red from where she had threatened to choke me to death, and my head was still hurting from when I hit the floor. I had scratches too, from where I tried to shield the blows that were violently coming at me.

As I looked at myself in the mirror, I was so ashamed and hurt by what my mother had done to me. I cried for a long time, and I could hear her standing outside the door of the bathroom. Yet, she didn't say anything. I remember hearing her walk away, and I started crying all over again.

Eventually, she would come to my room and say that she was sorry and that she hated to whip me, and that whipping me hurt her more than it hurt me. I couldn't see how that was possible, since I had bruises all over my upper body, and was still having trouble breathing, and my head was still throbbing, while she was standing there smoking a cigarette.

It was all because I told a lie.

I used to lie because I was afraid to tell the truth. Sometimes, her reaction to the truth was worse than her reaction to a lie. I couldn't win for losing, and it all depended on what kind of mood she was in.

One day I got slapped because she asked me where something was, and I didn't know. She accused me of taking it, but I wasn't a child who stole things. She slapped me, and I immediately left her presence and ran to the bathroom to cry and put cold water on my face.

A few minutes later, she was standing outside the door of the bathroom, apologizing because she had found what she was looking for, and had slapped me for no reason, but she had a bad day.

I was determined to do nothing that would make my mother mad enough to have to hit me. I was determined to tell the truth, no matter what the punishment, because at least I knew that if she was hitting me, or beating me, that I didn't deserve what I was getting, and I hoped that God would make her feel that much worse when she found out she beat me for no reason.

I am a person who is determined not to take my frustrations out on my child the way my mother took hers out on me.

MY SANDWICH

I grew up in Mississippi, and was an adventurous, sometimes stubborn child. I was a tough little boy, who had a mind of determination and a strong willed character.

I remember one time my mother told me to clean my room and I didn't want to. I was determined that I wasn't going to clean my room, and no matter what my mother said, she couldn't make me do it. My mother kept nagging, and nagging about me cleaning up my room, and as much as I tried to ignore her, she would not leave me alone.

Finally, I gave in, because my mother was more stubborn and strong willed than I and had I not given in, I would have gotten a whooping!

While I was cleaning my room, I mumbled to myself, "I don't wanna clean up my room!" For some reason, although I didn't have any problem messing the room up, I had a big problem with cleaning it up. However, while I was cleaning up what I messed up, I got the idea that I was going to run away from home to teach my mother a lesson for making me clean up my room. I wanted to hurt her, because she was making me clean up my mess. So, as I cleaned up, I packed. I cleaned some more, then packed some more.

While I was cleaning and packing, I started to get hungry. My stomach was growling, and with every movement of packing and cleaning, all I began to think about was food.

Suddenly, my mother called my name. It was lunchtime! She had fixed me a sandwich. But, being the stubborn, little tough guy that I was, who was mad because she made me clean up my room, I yelled back, "I'm not hungry!"

My mother informed me that my sandwich would be waiting for me on the table when I was finished cleaning my room. I didn't need her sandwich. I was determined that I was running away, and tough guys didn't eat their mother's sandwiches when they were running away.

After I finished putting away all of my toys, I grabbed a pillow case, you know like I saw the kids on TV do when they were running away, and filled it with a shirt, a pair of pants and a few of my favorite toys.

I crept through the house, so that no one would hear me. However, as quiet as I tried to be, the floor kept creaking. I thought my mother was going to hear me, and then my plan would be ruined. But just as I passed the kitchen, I spotted the sandwich my mother had left on the table for me. My stomach was still growling, and although I had tried to ignore it, my stomach seemed to be just as stubborn as I was. My senses started double teaming me. My eyes were staring at the sandwich, and my mouth began to water. My mind started telling me that I was a tough guy, and tough guys didn't eat their mother's sandwiches. I was going to run away, and I didn't need her sandwich to survive. My eyes kept staring at the sandwich on the table. My stomach continued to talk to me, and my mouth was watering. I looked around to see if my mother was coming. Before I knew it, I snatched that sandwich off the plate, and ran out the door. I was a tough guy, but I was a hungry tough guy.

As I ran through the yard and hid in the bushes, I felt empowered! I had done what I had been determined to do. I had run away, into the backyard, and no one, not even my mother, could make me clean up my room. I ate my sandwich, it was so good, then laid back on the grass, and thought about my new found freedom.

Eventually, I went back inside, but for a little while, I had accomplished a great thing by running away from home. The sad part about it was that no one had even realized that I had run away, they thought I had just gone outside to play!

That was one of the fondest memories I have of growing up. Now, as a grown man, a husband, a father, a grandfather, a brother, a professor, a volunteer coach and mentor, I still have the determination and strong willed characteristics I had as a small child.

I raise my children to strive for excellence in school, sports and other extracurricular activities, and do positive things that will benefit them in the future.

I encourage the young children on my little league football team to be determined to play hard, and even if they don't win, be proud that they played hard.

I have faced a lot of challenges in my life. My family wasn't rich growing up, so I was determined that my children would have more than I did. My wife and I have had to live check to check at times, but God always made a way for us. We had to struggle some, and juggle some while trying to raise a family and finish college, but we never missed a meal, even if it was a sandwich. I have faced racism on various forms throughout my life, and even now, as I work for a college that has a lot of subtle hidden racial issues.

I believe that excuses are unacceptable. I believe that if there are road blocks, we must find a way to go around them, or over them, under them, or through them.

As a man, who believes that God has always made a way for me to obtain great blessings, I know that being determined to accomplish goals is important. I know that God has a plan and a purpose for my life, therefore I work hard to show that I appreciate every blessing that comes my way. God gives to us so that we can be a blessing to others. He gives us not just tangible things, but He gives us knowledge that we can share with others.

I know that I am the master of my fate, and the captain of my destiny, and with much determination and much prayer, comes much power.

The task before us is never greater than the power behind us, and I am a man who is determined to be happy and fulfilled with life, because God has placed so many opportunities in my path.

THE LIGHT BULB MOMENT

I sat at the table, frustrated. With tears in my eyes, I tried to figure it out. The harder I thought, the more frustrated I became, but I just couldn't figure it out. Every time I reworked the problem, it came out wrong. I had erased my work so many times, that the eraser was worn down on my pencil.

The worst part was that my mother was standing in the kitchen talking about my light bulb not coming on. Ooooh! I hated when she talked about the light bulb. I didn't care about that stupid light bulb coming on. I had been sitting at the kitchen table for five hours doing math homework, and I was ready to pull my hair out!

My mom used to say that people had a light bulb moment when they finally understood something that was difficult. With math, there were many days that I sat at the kitchen table hoping for a light bulb moment that took hours to come. Yet, my mother was determined that I would not get up from the table until the light bulb moment occurred. I wished she would be like other parents who didn't care if their children did their homework or not. She had rules though. I had to bring home every book from every subject I had in school everyday. No TV before homework was finished, and no phone calls while doing homework. No messy homework would be turned in, and she had to check everything before it was turned in the next day.

My back used to hurt! I was the only kid on the school bus with a book bag that had all of their books in it. I went through at least three or four book bags every school year because the straps weren't sturdy enough to hold all of my books for the one hundred and ninety something days we were required to attend school. I don't think the makers of the book bags anticipated that a student would have a parent who would require them to carry five school books, that each had five hundred or more pages in it, plus a notebook, and a library book home everyday. Back then, backpacks weren't that popular.

My mother was a good student when she was in school. She was salutatorian of her graduating class, and said that she would have been valedictorian, if it wasn't for the fact that the teacher's daughter was in her senior class, and they chose her to be valedictorian so that she could get the scholarship that was being offered to college. That little scenario made life hard for me, because my mom was determined that I was going to college.

Now, I was nowhere close to being valedictorian or salutatorian, but I was a good student, and I was driven, and determined to make A's and B's in school. I got my first F in Texas History in the seventh grade because my teacher was a coach who didn't teach us anything. He just wrote notes on the overhead for us to copy every class period and then we were supposed to study them and take a test. I had never had a teacher like him before, so his teaching technique was baffling to me. However, after that first devastation in the form of an F appeared on my report card, I made an A in his class every report card after that. I was determined that no F's would appear on my report card.

One of my favorite teacher's in school was the typical example of what a teacher was like. She was older, she dressed conservatively, she wore her hair up, she wore her glasses on a chain that hung around her neck, and she was mean. Her favorite saying was, "If you always act like a fool, then you will be a fool!"

She never had to say that to me, because for one, my mother didn't play. However I did hear her tell students who were acting up in her class that statement at least several times a week.

Because my mother was strict on me when it came to my education, I have always been very determined at whatever I do to do my best. My mother used to say, "If a task is once begun, never leave it til' it's done. Tho' the task be great or small, do it well or not at all." That was her way of reminding me to do things right the first time, and if I wasn't going to do it the right way, then don't bother doing it at all.

I'm sure that this was something she learned when she was in school, because she remembered a lot of things her teacher said to the students that made her strive for excellence: "Use your brain for more than just to part your ears," "Knowledge is something that no one can take away from you.

Once you get it, it's yours." "Wash high as possible, wash low as possible, and then wash *possible*!"Her favorite, I believe was "You run, you rip, you run, you rip, you run, you rip and you stink."

Now that I am an adult, I am still determined to do my best at whatever I set out to accomplish. I am grateful for the teachers I had through the years who took the time to teach their students, not only book knowledge, but life knowledge. I believe that those life knowledge lessons are the one's that stick with us well into our adulthood because we are able to recall them at any given moment when telling a story about our past. I may not be able to tell you everything my favorite teacher taught me, but I can tell you her favorite phrases, the shade of lipstick she wore, the number of days she missed from work, and the positive things she said to me that made me be a better student, and a productive adult.

I still have light bulb moments, as my mother used to say, and I still get frustrated by life's issues from time to time. I still don't like math, but it is my desire to always be just as determined to do any task set before me, as I am to finish reading a good book.

I have realized that God never gives us more than we can handle, and for every dilemma that is in need of a light bulb moment, God is working it out. We just have to pray about it, sit quietly, and wait, and the answer that we are in need of will come. That answer from Him, is a light bulb moment.

Seek ye first the kingdom of God and His righteousness, and all things will be added unto you.- Matthew 6:33

REASON, SEASON OR LIFETIME

Email. What an amazing invention. Something that wasn't heard of when I was growing up, is now a daily routine for me. Junk mail, bills, chain emails, reminders, FaceBook invites, solicitations, requests, responses, forwarded messages…most of them I delete.

Every now and then, an email comes my way that makes sense and I save it, print it out, and even forward it to my favorite people. One such email was entitled, *"Reason, Season or Lifetime"*.

People come into your life for a reason, a season, or a lifetime. When you figure out which one it is, you will know what to do for each person.

> *When someone is in your life for a REASON . . . It is usually to meet a need you have expressed. They have come to assist you through a difficulty, to provide you with guidance and support, to aid you physically, emotionally, or spiritually. They may seem like a godsend, and they are! They are there for the reason you need them to be. Then, without any wrong doing on your part, or at an inconvenient time, this person will say or do something to bring the relationship to an end. Sometimes they die. Sometimes they walk away. Sometimes they act up and force you to take a stand. What we must realize is that our need has been met, our desire fulfilled, their work is done. The prayer you sent up has been answered. And now it is time to move on.*

When people come into your life for a SEASON . . .
It is because your turn has come to share, grow, or learn. They
bring you an experience of peace, or make you laugh. They
may teach you something you have never done. They usually
give you an unbelievable amount of joy. Believe it! It is real!
But, only for a season.

LIFETIME relationships teach you lifetime lessons; things
you must build upon in order to have a solid emotional
foundation. Your job is to accept the lesson, love the person,
and put what you have learned to use in all other relationships
and areas of your life. It is said that love is blind but friendship
is clairvoyant. -Author Unknown

This email was so amazing, that it spoke to my heart. I quickly shared it with my favorite people, even printed out a copy for keeps. More importantly, I saved it, for future references. From time to time I would reread it. I even had conversations with others about what it meant to them. It was just that powerful.

I have always thought myself to be a really good friend. I try to be the kind of friend that I want others to be to me. I respect others, pray for others, share my last, and try to be what God asks of us in Ephesians 4:32, kind, tenderhearted and forgiving.

As a child, I grew up surrounded by love. Not that my family was perfect, because no one grows up in a perfect household, but my family encouraged me and inspired me to achieve greatness in life.

My friends that I grew up with, are still my friends. Friends from college, are still my friends. So, I have to say that I have been blessed to have *LIFETIME* friendships.

When I decided to marry my husband, the word divorce was one that I never planned to use. Being a product of divorce, I was determined to make my marriage a *LIFETIME* marriage.

Before that email ever came to me, the concept of making relationships last was embedded in my heart.

Friends come in all shapes, sizes, colors, religious affiliations, personalities and from many backgrounds. I remember hearing someone say that we don't choose our friends, fate chooses them for us.

We form friendships on our jobs, at church, with our children's friend's parents, with our hair dresser and even our neighbors. We never know where they will come from. Sometimes, we don't even realize that a friendship is forming. It just evolves.

For every friendship I have formed, I have been determined to be the best friend that I can be. Although I realize that not all friendships are lasting, my heart breaks whenever someone I truly believed would be apart of my life for the rest of my life, fades away.

I had a friend. A really good friend. We did almost everything together. Our children hung out with each other. Our husbands hung out with each other. We were always on the phone or at each others home. It was a perfect friendship. I thought.

Then, *it* happened.

And *it*, drove a wedge between us, and our families, demolishing our friendship.

What is *it*? *It* is the junk that develops from misunderstandings, confusion, misspoken words, unkind actions, untrue statements. *It. It* is the drama and ugliness that develops, and works its way into the crevices of our relationships with others.

The specific details are not important. The fact that after some time had passed, and I tried to mend what was broken, is important. My intentions failed, and I was minus someone in my life that I had shared so many fun and positive moments with. Although I was determined to fix and hold on to a friendship that wasn't meant to be a *LIFETIME* friendship, God knew what was best for me.

God continued to show me that it was time for me to move on, and let go. He began to plant new seeds of friendship in my life, and reminded me of the friends I had that were indeed *LIFETIME* friendships. He showed me the *REASON* for the friendship that had faded away, and encouraged me to understand that although the *SEASON* of the friendship that was formed had run it's course, I would still have a *LIFETIME* of memories.

I am determined to encourage my children to be good, speak kind words, think positive thoughts, be respectful and honest, love everybody, yet don't allow anybody to use them. I am determined to teach my children that friendships are important and that it's okay to let go of friendships that are damaging to their heart.

Proverbs 17:17 teaches that a friend loves at all times. I am determined to carry that thought in my heart as I cherish the special people that God has placed in my life. I am determined to be a great wife, a great mother, a great person, who is a beautiful friend, regardless of the *reason* or the *season*, because we never know when our *lifetime* will come to an end.

GOD SENT ME AN ANGEL

I am a hard working man. I have a family, a wife and kids. I was raised in the church, went to church every Sunday, and whenever the doors of the church were open, and sang in the choir. My parents instilled in me the value of being a hard worker, a generous giver, a Christian, a good person, and a good father. They did this by being an example for me every day.

I have always been determined to be a fair person, and to be the type of man that God would have me to be.

I have my own business. I am a mechanic, and the only legitimate black mechanic in a small town.

One day, I was alone in my shop working on a car. I was underneath it, and it fell on top of me, crushing me. I couldn't reach the phone, and no one was around to hear me cry out for help.

Since I grew up in the church, and learned at an early age about prayer, I immediately began to talk to God.

I don't know how long I had been laying there, my body beginning to go numb, but out of nowhere, a white man appeared. I don't know who he was and had never seen him before, and being in a small town, I know everybody.

The man talked calmly to me, as he lifted the car up, and helped me from underneath it.

Then, as quickly and mysteriously as he came, he disappeared.

I had a few broken ribs, but was otherwise okay. I thank God for sending me an angel to save my life. I am determined to live each day of my life worthy to receive the miracles, signs and wonders that God has just for me.

When I share my story with others, some are amazed, while some doubt me, but I will always know in my heart that God sent me an angel.

FLAT TIRES

I was a sophomore in college. I was a good student, studied some, partied little, made friends easily.

I had my own apartment, and from time to time, would invite friends over to play games, eat and watch movies.

Of course, there were a lot of guys on campus. Cute ones, not so cute ones, tall ones, short ones, in-between ones, fine ones, fat ones, and way too skinny ones. Players, wanna-be-players, scholars, athletes, freeloaders. Nice ones, mean ones, conceded ones, arrogant ones, down to earth ones, and too-good-to-be-true ones. There were the ones who treated me like a little sister, the ones who were trying to see how far they could get with me, and the ones who knew not to even think about trying to talk to me, because they were not my type.

I became friends, or so I thought, with a guy who was one of the cute ones. He was fun to be around, didn't seem like a bad person, and so I didn't mind hanging out with him.

One evening, during pledge season, he came to my apartment looking for a place to hide because his fraternity brothers had been really giving him a hard time. We talked for a long time, watched television, and when it was time to go to sleep, I handed him a pillow and a blanket, and told him he could sleep on the sofa. We said goodnight, and I returned to my room, and closed the door.

I woke up startled because something was tugging on my underwear. I realized the guy I thought was my friend, the one I had allowed to sleep on my sofa, was on top of me. I started pushing him away and telling him no. But he put his weight on my body, held my hands with one hand and managed to pry my legs apart with the other. He then proceeded to rape me.

Tears rolled down my face, as I lay there, repeating the word *no*, over and over.

When he finished, he kissed me on my forehead, then headed to the bathroom to take a shower.

I couldn't move. I just, lay there. After he left, I cried.

After a few hours, I managed to take a shower, get dressed, and cry some more. It was a bad day. I didn't want to eat, or drink. I did, however, cry myself to sleep.

There was a knock on my door.

It was my neighbor. I didn't feel like being bothered, so I tried to ignore her. Since my car was parked outside, she knew that I was there, so she kept knocking. Finally, I went to the door.

I must have looked a hot mess, because the look on her face was unforgettable. She immediately asked me what happened. Not knowing if I should share my personal information with her, I tried to brush her off, so that she would go away. It didn't work. She walked right on in, folded her arms, and looked at me as if to say she wasn't leaving until I told her what was wrong.

I started crying again. She started questioning me.

"Did someone die? You got a bad grade? You in pain? Did someone hurt you?"

I just looked at her. "Did someone *hurt* you!"

My face turned red.

"Did someone rape you?" she walked over to me, and hugged me.

She asked me who did it, and what I planned to do about it. I didn't know what to do. Honestly.

I knew that rape was something that could portray a victim as if she asked for what happened. I knew that rape was a he said/she said kind of issue.

She stayed for a while, then had to leave to go take care of something she said. She promised not to say anything to anyone about the rape.

The next day, another friend came to visit me. She said that my neighbor told her that I was sick and that it would be a good idea for her to come check on me.

I was surprised when I opened the door to find her standing there. She knew right away that something was wrong, and because I knew her, I felt comfortable enough to share with her what had happened.

She was so upset. She started talking about killing him, or having her boyfriend and his friends beat him up. She coerced me to leave my apartment and go to her dorm with her to get some fresh air. I didn't want to go because I didn't want to see people. I was embarrassed and ashamed of what had happened. I felt that I was stupid for being trusting and allowing him to sleep in my apartment because he had not *seemed* like a rapist.

We went to my friend's room, where she changed clothes, and suddenly decided that we needed to go to the men's dorm to see if her boyfriend was there. He was best friends with one of the members of the fraternity the guy who raped me was on line for. I was not trying to bump into him, so I felt that it was a really bad idea to go to the men's dorm.

She grabbed her pocket knife as we headed out the door. She said she always carried it with her for protection.

When we got to the parking lot of the men's dorm, my friend had this look on her face. I couldn't imagine what she was thinking, but I knew it couldn't be good.

Before I knew it, she ran over to his car that she saw in the parking lot. She disappeared for only a few minutes, but when she came back, she had the biggest grin on her face. She looked at me and said, "He won't be going anywhere tonight. He will be here to receive his butt whooping tonight."

My friend didn't play!

She wanted to sit on the hill for awhile, just to see what would happen when he got ready to leave.

We waited there for about an hour, just talking, trying to get my mind off of my issue.

Then, we saw him, and three of his line brothers headed to his car. They backed out of the parking space, drove out of the parking lot, but then the car suddenly stopped. All four doors of the car opened up. As he walked around his car, his friends burst into laughter. We could hear him cursing, as we sat perched inconspicuously on the hill. All four of his tires were flat.

I had to admit that it did make me feel better to see him unhappy at that moment.

That wasn't the end of it.

We went inside the men's dorm and waited for her boyfriend to come.

When he finally showed up, she pulled him to the side and told him what happened to me. His eyes got so wide. His previously glad to see his girlfriend smile, had turned into an angry mug. He clinched his fists, and began to look around as if he was looking for someone.

He told his girlfriend to walk me back to my apartment, and that he was going to make sure that the guy who raped me got punished.

Later that night, there was a knock at my door. It was late, and I definitely was leery about letting someone in after what had happened just the night before.

I peeked through the peephole. It was a friend that was like a brother to me. He and his brother considered themselves my bodyguards.

I opened the door slowly, to be met with the question, "That little punk raped you?"

I looked at him, nodded my head, and felt my eyes fill with tears.

He moved closer to me, hugged me, and said not to worry, because he was going to take care of the situation personally.

I didn't see the guy who raped me for a few days. However, I heard from several sources that he couldn't walk very well. You see, at the college I attended, hazing was real. Fraternity's hit pledges with paddles, punched them, and made them run for long distances. They made them do all kinds of embarrassing and unimaginable things you read about or see in the movies. From my understanding, they took turns beating the mess out of him, and spelled the word rapist as the beat him. He was then kicked off line.

Determined not to be the reason some other trusting young woman was raped by him, I went to the Dean and told him what happened. He called the guy in, questioned him, and after an investigation, the guy was suspended from school.

I am determined to not be too trusting. I am determined to not relive that night. I am determined to encourage others who have been raped to tell someone who can help them, so that rapists don't go free, freely preying on other women, raping them, and taking away their power.

No means *no*, and victims of rape must be determined to overcome the situation that for a moment, left them feeling powerless.

MY KNEES HIT THE FLOOR

All of my life, I have been committed to serving the Lord. I was raised in the church, and I go to church several times a week. When I'm not in church, I am somewhere talking about how good God has been to me.

I am married, with children and grandchildren. I am a hard working woman, who doesn't let things worry me, because I know that God is in control of my life.

Having a relationship with God is the best decision I have ever made. If it wasn't for him, I know that I could not have made it through some of the hardest times in my life. I have always been determined to have faith, and I have always trusted that God would work everything out in His own way, and in His own time.

Many years ago, my daughter was found raped and murdered. She had been missing for several days, and when my knees hit the floor, I prayed for her safe return. But, God had other plans. When the police came to notify me that they had found my daughter's body, I almost passed out. I cried, and I prayed to God to give me the strength I needed to not let her murder break me. I had flashbacks, to when she was born. I remembered the day she walked for the first time and I remembered the first words she spoke. I recalled her smile and the last words we spoke.

The police never charged anyone with her murder.

Twenty years later, another one of my daughters was found raped and murdered. It was like déjà vu. As much as I love the Lord, I was still hurting inside. When my knees hit the floor, I didn't question why God had taken my daughter's lives, I prayed for strength to deal with the test that God had placed in my path. Just like before, the police never charged anyone with her murder either.

Of course, it hurt that two of my children had met cruel and violent deaths, and had spent the last moments of their lives with someone who meant them harm. It hurt me to know that the last words they heard were unkind words, and the last set of eyes that met theirs, were filled with hate and evil. It hurt me to know that they died alone, in an unfamiliar place, with no one they loved there to protect them. It hurt me to know that someone on this earth, who had no regard for life, for peace, for respect of others, had crossed my daughter's paths, and brought to end the life that God gave to them.

My knees hit the floor everyday. I thank God for giving me peace of mind, and for taking care of my other children.

I carry my Bible everywhere I go and I actually study the words written on those pages. I share the goodness of God with others, and encourage others to try God. I have met all kinds of people, but I never look down on anyone for whatever problems they may have. I pray for them, and remind them that God can take care of them, and change their lives if they give him a chance.

When people see me, they always see a smile on my face. God has been too good for me to walk around sad, with a frown on my face.

I think back sometimes to those moments of sadness, and despair, of losing two children in such a horrible, horrible way. Yet, I know that if it wasn't for God being the head of my life, and the fact that I remember to pray every morning, and every night, and several times in between, I never would have made it. I am determined to always love God, trust God, lean on God, and depend on God, because without Him, I would be nothing.

A WIFE & KIDS?

As I sit quietly sometimes, I think of how simple my life used to be. Back before I met her, before the children, before there were no toys and noise, no dogs or cats, no family car or neighborhood kids running through our home and yard.

It was just me. A single man, who never really thought about having a family. A wife and kids? Me? I wasn't too sure about that. I enjoyed my alone time, and not having to yell at kids, and not having to compromise with anyone.

I used to see people in the store, and see kids throwing tantrums in the aisles. I would watch in amazement at how parents would allow their kids to kick and scream, and not do anything about it. I would get so mad because I just couldn't imagine why they were allowing their kids to act like brats.

Then, I met her. At the grocery store, of all places. She was very beautiful, and had an enchanting smile. She was so polite, and it seemed like we hit it off immediately.

We began to see each other and I looked forward to the time we spent together. There was one problem; she had children.

I won't say that it was really a problem, but it was kind of difficult dating her, and dealing with someone else's, some other man's children. We had different views on how to deal with them. Me, being a man, I was stern, while she, being a woman, had a calming, soothing, and patient way in which she dealt with them.

Since I loved her, I tried to make things work. I missed her when time

105

insisted that we be apart, and I looked forward to the moments when I knew we would be together.

Sometimes, my stubbornness would cause tension in our relationship. I was just used to doing things my own way, and I imagine that she was used to doing things her own way.

I found myself giving in more and more as time went by, and I realized that I became less and less stubborn. I recall someone saying that love changes you. It changes how you act, how you think, how you feel, how you react, how you speak, how you live. When you really love someone, you no longer worry about you, and whether things are always your way. You worry about your mate, and how your actions will affect them. You think of them before you think of yourself, and the simplest things remind you of them.

A wife and kids? I have to admit, I would have never thought I would be able to say that I had either of those in my life. I was used to living my life, without having to consider anyone's feelings but my own.

Tall, dark, handsome and mysterious. Those are words that I used to hear people say when they described me. Now, husband and dad have replaced them.

I used to be determined not to allow anyone to get too close to me. I felt that it was best because I was a very private person.

I have met a few really good people in my life. Some that I have adopted as my family. One of them, would always tell me how different it is when you have your own children. She said that I would think differently, and be a lot more lenient and patient with my own child than I was with other people's children.

When our son was born, it was the most amazing thing I have ever experienced. To see this tiny human being come into the world, without a care in the world, I must admit my heart began to soften. Then I saw traces of me in him. My eyes, my toes, my ears. There was this mini version of me, wrapped up in this tiny package I was holding in my arms.

I was determined that I would be a great dad. I would remember things that my own dad taught me as I grew up. I would remember things my mother did for me, songs she sang to me. It was now my turn to pass these things on to my son.

As each day passes, I realize what my friend was saying to me, when she said I would become more lenient and more patient, when she would tell me that I would have to give in sometimes, even when I didn't want to, just to make things work. I can see that there are times when I am very nurturing and easy going, and not just with my son, but with my wife, and my stepsons too.

I must confess that although my life used to be very simple, before my wife and kids came along, I wouldn't go back to those days if given the chance. There are so many things that I have been able to experience now, that I would not have had the opportunity to experience if I was single, and childless.

Some of the simplest things in life, like hearing a baby's heart beat for the first time, the miracle of childbirth, or a child crawling into your lap for you to read to them, or children squirting water on you while giving the dog a bath, or watching the kids play baseball or basketball, or teaching a small child to ride a bike.

I am thankful to God for so many things, but one thing I am most thankful for is the way He allowed me to open up my heart, so that I could experience what true love is like, with my wife and kids.

I am determined to be a great husband and a great dad.

THEY GET ON MY NERVES

Tuesday Night

Ooooh, my parents get on my nerves. They think they know everything, just because they are my parents.

Do this, and do that. Don't say this, and don't say that. Don't wear this, and don't listen to that. Oh my gosh! All they do is nag.

I will be so glad when I get out on my own. I won't have to do chores, and I won't have to listen to them nagging me all of the time.

I am practically grown. I can make my own decisions. I don't need them to do nothing for me.

I wonder what's for dinner.

Ooooh! She's calling my name again. What does she want now? Probably wants me to come do something stupid, like fold the towels. Why can't she fold them? She bought them.

Uhhhhh! He's calling my name. Probably wants me to go get him something to drink. Why can't he get it? All he's doing is sitting on his butt, watching football. He is so lazy. He can get up and get it himself.

Boyfriend's text:	"what r u doin"
My text:	"nothin"
Boyfriend's text:	"u wanna go 2 the movies Saturday"
My text:	"i have 2 ask my parents"
Boyfriend's text:	"ok"

My text:	"hold on"
My text to mama:	"Mama, can I go 2 the movies with my friends Saturday?"
Mama's text:	"Which friends?"
My text to mama:	"lisa & kim"
Mama's text:	"We'll see. Depends on your attitude this week, & whether or not you get your chores done."

Ooooh. She gets on my nerves! Always talking about my attitude! I don't have an attitude.

My text to mama:	"yes ma'am"
My text to daddy:	"Daddy, can I go 2 the movies with my friends Saturday?"
Daddy's text:	"Ask your mama"

Dang. He gets on my nerves. Why can't he just say yes. Why does he always tell me to ask her?

My text:	"she said she will see. I'll let you know Friday."
Boyfriend's text:	"ok"
My text:	"what r u doin"
Boyfriend's text:	"playin video games"
My text:	"ok"

There she goes calling my name again.

Come do the dishes? Dang. Why do I have to do the dishes? I didn't cook.

Why does she have to cook with every pot and pan in the kitchen? Why does he get a different cup every time he gets something to drink? Ooooh! They get on my nerves.

<u>Wednesday Morning</u>

Ooooh! She gets on my nerves. I am moving as fast as I can. I'm trying to fix my hair. Gotta look good for school.

I don't know who she thinks she is talking to. She must be crazy. She ain't gon do nothing. Ain't like she can just leave me.

I can't believe he made me go change my clothes! Talking about my skirt was too short! It was this short when we bought it from the store!

What? She's in there talking about we bought it last year, and that I have grown since then. Whatever!

Ooooh! Why does she have to talk every time we get in the car.

Man, that's my song on the radio. And she won't shut up!

I can't even hear the words, because she is getting on my nerves, talking! Talk! Talk! Talk!

Man, I missed it.

I asked her if I could go to the movies with my friends Saturday. She acted like she didn't hear me.

I'm glad I'm at school, so I don't have to hear her mouth.

"Mama, can I have some lunch money?"

<u>Wednesday Night</u>

I asked her if I could go to the movies Saturday with my friends.

She said I sure was determined to go to the movies, then she asked me if I had finished my homework.

Why is she worrying about me doing my homework?

"No sir, I'm not texting while I'm doing my homework?"

Boyfriend's text:	"What r u doin"
My text:	"Watchin tv"
Boyfriend's text:	"What r u wearin"
My text:	"Clothes"
Boyfriend's text:	"Send me a pic"
My text:	"ok"
Boyfriend's text:	"Nice pic"

My text:	"Send me a pic of u"
Boyfriend's text:	"ok"
My text:	"Nice pic"
Boyfriend's text:	"Where r ur parents"
My text:	"N the other room"
Boyfriend's text:	"Send me a pic of u without clothes"
My text:	"Huh?"
Boyfriend's text:	"Come on, I won't let anybody else see it"
My text:	"I don't know"
Boyfriend's text:	"I'll send u one of me"
My text:	"Ok. U go first"
Boyfriend's text:	"Ok."

My mom walked in just as I sent the picture of myself, naked. She is going crazy! I don't think I have ever seen her that mad before.

I don't know what the big deal is. She is really just overreacting.

My dad is yelling at me. I wish he would be quiet. Ooooh! He gets on my nerves. Ok, I hear you. You keep saying the same thing over and over.

Yes! It's finally over. I get to go to my room.

WHAT! I know she didn't just make me give her my phone!

She gets on my nerves!

She has a belt in her hand. I am too old to get a whooping! Whatever, she better not hit me!

Dang! She hit me HARD! My hands hurt cause I was trying to keep her from hitting my butt. My butt hurts too. At first, I wasn't going to cry. But she kept hitting me, so I couldn't help my self.

Ooooh! She get's on my nerves! HOW MANY MORE LICKS IS SHE GOING TO GIVE ME!?!?

I knew it was wrong when he asked me to send him the picture of myself without any clothes on, but I wasn't thinking.

I can't believe she took my phone.

My parents said they can't trust me now.

It was just a harmless picture. No big deal. He said he wasn't going to show it to anyone.

Dang. I can't text anybody now. What am I going to do? I guess I will do my homework.

Man, my butt is sore.

Thursday Morning

I asked my mama if I could go to the movies Saturday with my friends. She just looked at me like she wanted to knock my head off.

I asked her when I could have my phone back, and her head spun around like the girl from the *Exorcist* movie.

Boys were looking at me and smiling? Boys I didn't even like.

Ooooh. A group of girls, that didn't even like me, were staring at me. They were getting on my nerves.

One of my friends said she tried to text me, but I explained to her that my parents took my phone away. She said she received a text message with a picture of me, naked!

I don't understand. The only person who had a naked picture of me was, my boyfriend!

Oh, no! He promised he wouldn't show anyone else!

My friend said that the picture was all over school.

I suddenly became ill. The thought of everyone in school seeing a picture of me, naked, made me feel so embarrassed.

I realized at that moment, what my parents were so mad about.

Boys were walking by me, making nasty comments. Girls were looking at me and pointing, and I knew they were talking about me.

I just wanted to cry!

I went to the school nurse, but she said that since I didn't have a fever, I wasn't sick. She got on my nerves too. Why did I have to have a fever to be sick? Why couldn't she just look at my eyes, that were red because I had been crying, and let me call my mama so I could go home.

I wanted to go home! I didn't want to go through the rest of the day being stared at, and humiliated.

When I saw my boyfriend, I asked him why did he send my picture to everybody. He said it was an accident. He said he was trying to send something else, but my picture got sent instead.

I wanted to claw his eyes out!

He apologized, but for some reason, I didn't think he was sincere.

Then, he asked me if I was going to the movies with him Saturday, and if not, he was going to ask someone else.

I felt my head begin to spin around like the girl from the *Exorcist* movie. If he only knew how much trouble I was in because of him, and he head the nerve to say he was going to ask someone else to go if I couldn't!

I was determined not to cry in front of him, so I just walked away.

Thursday Night

I don't want to be bothered. I don't want to eat. I just want to sleep.

Don't you see that my door is closed!

Quit calling my name! You are getting on my nerves!

I'm just going to lie here, and pretend to be sleep.

He's standing at the door.

Now she's standing at the door.

I guess the fact that my light is off and I am covered up doesn't mean anything to them. They want to talk. How rude!

My parents can be so mean sometimes. They don't understand what it's like to be a teenager. They didn't have computers and cell phones when they were growing up. They didn't have mp3 players, CDs, DVDs, or IPODS. I don't know how they made it.

For people my age, texting, internet and face book is a necessity. It's how we keep track of each other, and get all of the latest gossip on who did what and who said what.

I can't imagine how they made it without cell phones back then. I don't know what I would do if I couldn't text my friends. I would be so bored.

I make pretty good grades in school. My parents are never satisfied. They say I can do better, but there's nothing wrong with making B's, C's, and every once in a while, a D, or two. I go to church almost every Sunday, and I have favorite Bible scriptures.

They always talk about how good I have it, compared to other kids. They always say that I don't appreciate the things that they do so that I can live a good life. They get on my nerves with all of that talking.

They are taking away my computer privileges! What?

They are taking my ipod! What?

Uh oh! My dad read the text messages I sent to my boyfriend.

He found out that I was trying to go to the movies with my boyfriend instead of my friends. Dang. Here they go with another lecture. This one is about lying. Blah, blah, blah.

What did he just say?

I can't believe it! He responded to a text my boyfriend just sent me.

How embarrassing! I can't believe him. He had no right to do that! That was my phone. Just because they pay the bill, they think they can tell me what to do with it.

They get on my nerves!

What? Another whooping? For lying?

DANG! I can't wait until I'm grown! I am determined to hurry up and graduate so I can move out on my own, so I don't have to do what they say, or put up with their nagging and complaining and bossing me all of the time.

My daddy's whooping me this time! His whooping hurts worse than mamas. But he likes to talk when he whoops!

NO-SIR! I-WON'T-LIE-TO-YOU-AGAIN!!!

NO-SIR! I-WON'T-TAKE-NAKED-PICTURES-OF-MYSELF-AND-SEND-THEM-TO-ANYBODY!!!

YES-SIR!!! I-LEARNED-MY-LESSON!!!

YES-SIR!!! I-LEARNED-MY-LESSON!!!

SOMEBODY PRAYED FOR ME

The water was cold on my face. It was dark, and quiet. A few stars glimmered in a far off distance. Every now and then, I could hear a car engine in the distance and see remnants of headlights.

I was in so much pain. My clothes were soaked in blood.

As I lay there in the shallow water, apparently left for dead, my determination to live began to manifest.

It hurt more than any pain I had ever felt, but I managed to drag my injured, and bleeding body from the water. I headed towards the direction of the noises from the cars. It was the only way to get help. Every step I took was a struggle. It seemed to take forever to get to the road. I prayed to God to send me some help. I didn't want to die this way, in this cold, dark place, in the middle of nowhere, alone.

Finally, I saw the headlights of a car coming. I stood on the side of the road, attempting to flag the car down. It wasn't just any car. It was a police car.

I was a young, married father with a new baby. I was a soldier in the Army on leave. I had two choices that night, one was to go home to my wife, the other to hang out with my younger brother. Well, hanging out with my brother was so much more fun, so we drove around for awhile. Just talking and listening to music.

I enjoyed hanging out with him because he wasn't the same bratty little brother he used to be. He had grown out of the annoyance stage, and was now not just my brother, but also my homey.

We ended up at a club, where a girl approached me about giving her a ride. I agreed, and when I approached an intersection, a car came from behind and began to irritate me. Two guys got out of the car, and began walking towards mine. One of the guys was talking crazy and accusing me of messing with his girlfriend.

I felt threatened as I tried to explain why she was in my car. I went to the trunk to get my gun, but before I could use it, one of them shot me, and I was then beat up. They threw me in my car, and the two cars began a journey that I had no way of knowing where it would end.

Eventually, the guy who was driving my car stopped. He talked to the guy in the other car about what they were going to do, then opened the car door, and snatched me out of the car, like I was a bag of trash. My body was thrown by the water, maybe they intended for me to drown. I don't know. But they drove away, taking my car with them.

The highway patrol seemed shocked as he flashed his bright lights at me. I don't even remember if he pulled his car over to the side of the road. I just remember waking up in the hospital with tubes and beeping noises, and bright lights and doctors all around me.

I could hear them, but they couldn't hear me. They were talking about my chances of recovery and talking about a lot of medical stuff I didn't understand.

I remember seeing my wife's tear stricken face, and my mom's too. I knew that they were both scared and unsure of what to make of my predicament.

I was in and out of consciousness. I overheard somebody say that there were a lot of people in the waiting room praying for me.

It took me months to get well enough to go home. But although I was leaving the hospital, I was far from recovery.

My spleen had to be removed. Injuries from the assault left me a diabetic, and my immune system was very weak. At some point, my kidneys began to shut down, but I was determined to live, for my wife and my child.

The police found my car a few days later. It had been stripped and burned. They also found and arrested the guys and the girl who had set a trap for me to be carjacked.

We went to trial. They got some time. However, I have never been a person who hates others, or wishes to see evil come to them. I asked that the judge give them another chance. Although my life had been completely altered by what they did to me, shooting me, beating me, and leaving me for dead, I still didn't hate them. I had prayed for them, and about the situation. God had spared my life, and I asked the judge to do the same for theirs.

One of my attackers apologized for what they had done to me. I know I did the right thing by forgiving them. It was my hope and prayer that they would do the right thing, and stay out of trouble once they served the minimal sentences they received.

My near death experience brought my wife and I closer. My family, as a whole, including my mother and brother, grew closer.

I learned a lot from the experience, including the importance of taking care of yourself, and not giving up.

Doctors said I should have been dead. If the highway patrol had not come along when he did, I would have died on that lonely highway.

I often think back to the whisper I heard as I lay in ICU. Somebody whispered in my ear that people were praying for me to get better. I am glad that I had people in my life that were praying for me, because during that time, I couldn't pray for myself.

I am not healed. I will never be healed. I will always live with the memory of that night. When I wake up in the morning, unable to see because I have been declared legally blind due to the diabetes I developed from the injuries I sustained that night, I remember. When I wake up from a seizure, another ailment left behind from that night, I remember. When I look in the mirror at my once strong, muscular body, and see a thinner version of me, I remember. When I go to dialysis, I remember.

I remember wanting to give up. I remember thinking that I didn't like what I saw when I looked in the mirror. I remember feeling weak, and helpless. I hated having others wait on me, and drive me, and baby me. I hated taking all those pills, and visiting doctors every week. I missed not being able to work. I missed being the man my wife married. I missed, the old version of me.

I am glad that I will get to watch my children grow up to become adults. I am glad that I get to enjoy the important moments of life, like my son fixing me dinner, or my daughter making sure that daddy is ok. I enjoy spoiling them, and having important discussions with my son. I am proud that my daughter comes to me when she has a problem.

One good and important thing that I didn't lose in the midst of all the madness was my sense of humor. I still laugh everyday, and I mostly enjoy embarrassing my daughter when I see a young boy looking at her in a certain way. I will play crazy in a heart beat, or say something to let him know not to even think about talking to my daughter.

I know my wife gets tired sometimes. But I do appreciate her for loving me and not leaving me after everything happened. She has always been supportive, even when I have been hard to get along with.

I am a survivor, a forgiver, a husband, a father, a son, a brother and a friend who is determined to be here for every important event that is to come in the lives of my family and friends.

I am determined to not wallow in pity, or to be sad or depressed about my health issues. God has a plan for me. He saved my life for a reason, so there is no reason for me to complain.

I am determined to scare away as many of my daughter's male friends as I can. I am determined to one day walk them down the aisle. I am determined to see my son become a man, and start a family of his own. I am determined to be around long enough to hear somebody call me PaPa. I am determined to grow old and grey with my wife, and sit on the front porch, with nothing better to do, than watch the cars go by, and drink poly pop. I am determined to rebuild myself one day at a time. I am determined not to give up on myself, which will teach my children not to give up on themselves.

Someone asked me how could I forgive the people who altered my life. It had to be God, because only power that comes from Him could allow me to be so forgiving.

I have learned to look for the bright light, or positive, in every situation. I also learned to pray for others, just as somebody took the time to pray for me.

I WON'T COMPLAIN

From time to time, someone at church will resonate their rendition of a song that tells the story of a soul who has endured life's trials and tribulations. One such song that sticks out in my mind was written by Bishop William C. Abney, and made famous by a young thirty-year-old Pastor, Reverend Paul Jones, of Houston, TX. The song, entitled, *I Won't Complain* is so moving, that it tugs at the heart and soul, reminding me that it doesn't matter what the situation looks like at the moment, because God has taken care of me, and will continue to do so. If I close my eyes, I can hear these words, usually being delivered by a powerful voice…

I've had some good days
I've had some hills to climb
I've had some weary days
And some sleepless nights
But, o, when I look around
And I think things over
All of my good days
Outweigh my bad days
And I, won't complain
Sometimes the clouds hang low
I can hardly see the road
I ask the question, Lord
Lord, why so much pain?
But He knows what's best for me
Although my weary eyes
They cannot see

So I'll just say thank you Lord
And I won't complain.
The Lord has been so good to me
He's been good to me
More than this old world or you could ever be
He's been so good to me
He dried all of my tears away
Turned my midnights into day
So I'll just say thank you Lord
I've been lied on
But thank you Lord
I've been talked about
But thank you Lord
I've been misunderstood
But thank you Lord
You might be sick
Body reeking with pain
But thank you Lord
The bills are due
Don't know where the money's coming from
But thank you Lord...

A person who hasn't been through anything, might not be able to understand what those lyrics mean. My mother used to say, "You haven't experienced everything, but just keep living." Yet when she used to say that to me, I would think, "Ok." Not realizing what she was truly saying to me.

Then one day, I started living, and I truly began to see what my mother was talking about.

I believe that everything we experience, is done to teach us something. I believe that everything we experience is a test of our faith and courage. I believe that everything we experience is designed to strengthen us, and help us grow.

I have realized that the battle isn't easy, and I admit that from time to time, I have felt like giving up. Yet there is a still, small voice that I can hear, reminding me that God has my back and because He has my back, everything is going to be alright.

Who am I? Well, I am a survivor of rape.

Who am I? I am a person who was molested by a stranger as a child.

Who am I? I was a teenage mother.

Who am I? I am a survivor of physical abuse.

Who am I? I am a survivor of emotional abuse.

Who am I? I am a failure at marriage.

Who am I? I am a single mother.

Who am I? I am a single father.

Who am I? I am a victim of rumors.

Who am I? I am an orphan.

Who am I? I am a significant member of society.

Who am I? I am a victim of workplace drama.

Who am I? I am a lover of music.

Who am I? I am a person who is often misunderstood.

Who am I? I am a person who treats others the way I want to be treated.

Who am I? I am a person on a journey to peace.

Who am I? I am a caring individual who strives to see the good in everyone.

Who am I? I am a person who has gone without eating from time to time, so that my children could eat.

Who am I? I am a person who from time to time, wakes up in the wee hours of the morning, and has conversations with God.

Who am I? I am a person who enjoys children.

Who am I? I am a talented individual.

Who am I? I am a person who has made some bad choices in life.

Who am I? I am a person who knows that I cannot dwell on the negative choices, because they will keep me from getting to a positive place.

Who am I? I am beautiful, fearfully, and wonderfully made.

Who am I? I am a victim of stalking.

Who am I? I am a person who chose to live in isolation.

Who am I? I am a person who has given her last so that strangers could have.

Who am I? I am a defeater of depression.

Who am I? I am a survivor of life.

Who am I? I am a caretaker.

Who am I? I am a believer that what doesn't kill us, only makes us stronger.

Who am I? I am a person who believes that we should make friends who are life-timers.

Who am I? I am a believer that not everyone who is in our lives means us good.

Who am I? I am a lover of the simple things, like the beauty of stars in the sky, or butterflies on a beautiful spring day.

Who am I? I am a person who enjoys trying new things, and taking chances, because we only live once.

Who am I? I am a person who believes that God opens doors for us, and it is important that we are able to see the exit sign, so that we can walk through it.

Who am I? I am a person who is in awe every time I see a rainbow.

Who am I? I am a person who is motivated to do great things.

Who am I? I am a person who doesn't like excuses, so I look for ways to get things done.

Who am I? I am the topic of gossip.

Who am I? I am a mediator.

Who am I? I am a great listener.

Who am I? I am a great organizer.

Who am I? I am an individual who encourages others.

Who am I? I am a person who avoids negative people.

Who am I? I am a person who has a plan.

Who am I? I am an individual who knows what it's like to have bills that are due, and not know where the money came from to pay them.

Who am I? I am a person who has worked tirelessly on a job, only to be unappreciated by my employer.

Who am I? I am a person who has had four jobs at one time to pay my bills.

Who am I? I am a person who let stress creep into my life, and slowly weaken me.

Who am I? I am a person who did not like the way I looked on the outside.

Who am I? I am an example of strength, courage and wisdom.

Who am I? I am a person who has witnessed the nasty attitudes of Church people.

Who am I? I am a person who knows that there are plenty of devils in the Church pews.

Who am I? I am a person who would prefer to sit quietly at church on Sunday morning, yet God has other plans for me.

Who am I? I am a parent who has had to make sacrifices for her children.

Who am I? I am a parent who has been called mean by her children.

Who am I? I am a parent who has imperfect children.

Who am I? I am a parent who is loved by her children.

Who am I? I am a person who cries in my secret closet to God because I know that He is my comforter.

Who am I? I am an individual who has a heart for helping others.

Who am I? I am a penny pincher.

Who am I? I am an entrepreneur.

Who am I? I am a seeker of knowledge.

Who am I? I am a person who guards her heart so that it cannot be damaged.

Who am I? I am a person who has witnessed child abuse.

Who am I? I am a person who has experienced tragedies and heartaches, who has had a visit from disappointment, and a talk with despair.

Who am I? I am a person who has been spared from death, and allowed to continue along this journey called life.

Who am I? I am a person who lives with a mate who does not show me love.

Who am I? I am a person who does more for others, than others do for me.

Who am I? I am a person who reads between the lines.

Who am I? I am a person who lives in pain everyday.

Who am I? I am a person with a past that is hard to forget.

Who am I? I am a fighter.

Who am I? I am a person who prays for others.

Who am I? I am a person who prays for herself.

Who am I? I am a recipient of miracles.

Who am I? I am a person who walks in favor.

Who am I? I am a creation designed by God. I am a person who has determination and drive. I choose not to just accept the negative darts that are thrown my way. I find a way to block them. And if I can't block them, God has a way of letting them not pierce my heart! I might get nicked sometimes, but life's trials and tribulations don't knock me down.

Yes, I am a real person. I having feelings, faults, dreams and struggles. I am all those things rolled up and shaped into one single human being. My name isn't important, but my ability to overcome is.

When I got to the point in my life where I didn't complain about whatever it was that I was going through, the words to the song, "I Won't Complain" had new meaning. Yes, we talk about what's going on, what's bothering us with our real good friends. Sometimes, friends grow tired of listening, but the real good friends encourage you, and pray for you and with you. Sometimes, we have a good cry, but those tears that roll down our face should be a sign of trials and tribulations exiting our lives, so that strength, courage and wisdom may be restored.

If you found yourself in these pages, you are the epitome of determination. Your "I" situation is a blessing to others, so don't give up, don't stop praying, don't stop doing the things that will lead you to a calm and peaceful place. Remember, from every test we face, comes a testimony we can share with others.

PROMISE TO MYSELF

I will not let rumors destroy me
For they are only the product of small minds.
I will not let the word "hate" be a part of my life
Because that one word may hinder my entrance into heaven.
I will not let disappointments rule my life
For it is through disappointments that I will learn about life.
I will not give up on myself
But will be determined to love myself, and encourage myself.
I will not assume the worst
For in assuming the worst
I will become the worst.
I will not live only for myself
But will think of others as well.
For it is in being kind to others
That good things in return will happen to me.

SOMETHING EXTRA

Dear Reader:

I have been writing since I was thirteen-years-old. The remaining pages of this book are a selection of pieces that my mother and friends enjoyed the most. They expressed to me how much they wished they could have all their favorites in one place, in one book. So, here they are.

For those who saved my articles from the newspaper, thank you for your support and encouragement. It has always been my desire and determination to encourage others through words.

Miracles and Blessings to you...

Dear Friend,

I heard you say the other day that you didn't think you were pretty. You couldn't really give a reason, but said you were unhappy with some outer parts of your body. The fact that you cannot see beauty within yourself compelled me to write you this letter. Why? Because it's my job, as your friend to help you see how beautiful you are on the inside, so you'll understand how it makes you beautiful on the outside to others. You see, one must be beautiful internally. That's the most important part of a beautiful person.

You have a quiet spirit and a giving nature. You think of others before you think of yourself. You pray for others. You have sympathy for others and think of ways to help them. You have a personal relationship with God, and it shows. When you hear a song, you recognize the beauty in the words. You think of positive outcomes as blessings, not luck. You feel bad when you do something you know is wrong. You respect yourself, and others. Because you respect yourself, others respect you.

From these inner beauty attributes, comes your outer beauty. Someone was quoted for saying that beauty is in the eye of the beholder. When you look at yourself in the mirror, this is what you should see. Let's start with your beautiful eyes that see the good in others. They also see when others need help, and without having to be asked, you offer assistance. You see the beauty in simple things, like clouds and flowers, and find the things God made funny to make us laugh. With your mouth you often speak kindly of others. You speak positive things, and encourage others each day. Most importantly, you have a smile that radiates the essence of beauty. With your ears you listen attentively to what others have to say. You choose not to hear evil, and when you do, you pray for those who are speaking it.

Now, for that body that you believe is less than perfect, people come in all shapes and sizes. No two people are exactly alike. And everyone is unhappy with something. Some don't like the color of their eyes, or the color of their hair, while some think their lips are too thin, and others think their lips are too full. There's someone who thinks their fingers are too long, while someone else believes their fingers are too short. There is someone who thinks they are too thin, and needs to add a few pounds, while someone else thinks they are too heavy, and needs to shed a bunch of pounds. And what about that person who thinks that the beauty mark on their face is terribly disfiguring? Everyday someone else is applying a fake one to make themselves more beautiful.

With all due respect, beautiful one, I would know if you were ugly, because I'm with you everyday! Think about it, who else is with you when you are at your worst and best?

Sincerely,
Your Self Esteem

WHEN HE BECAME A MAN

He'd seen a lot.
He'd done a lot.
He'd been through a lot.
He'd begun to listen more.
He'd begun to dislike less.
His intentions...good, although sometimes misunderstood.
His objectives and motives...sometimes questionable.
His imperfections...often brought to light.
His dilemmas...often difficult to overcome.
His heart was in the right place.
His mind, full of positive thoughts.
His body, a well built temple.

He'd always tried to live by the creed set forth by Les Brown, who said, "If you fall, fall on your back. If you can look up, you can get up."

He'd come to agree with Minister Louis Farrakhan, who said, "You've got to get the mind cleared out before you put the truth in it."

He'd begun to view life the way Malcolm did when he said, "A man, who stands for nothing, will fall for anything."

He understood what James Baldwin meant when he said, "You cannot fix what you will not face."

Still, he was perplexed by Thurgood Marshall's question which asks, "What is the quality of your intent?"

From his mother, he'd learned to respect women.
From his father, he'd learned pride.
As a boy, he'd learned the rewards of being trustworthy.
As a young man, he'd learned the value of money.
As a son, he'd learned what it was like to be loved.
As a brother, he'd learned the importance of loyalty.
As a friend, he'd experienced the fulfillment of brotherhood.

All of these things were essential to adulthood.
Yet, it was when he learned to truly love himself-
When he learned to take responsibility for his own actions-
When he learned to be dependent on himself-
And when he learned not to judge others-
That he became a MAN!

ONE BIG FAMILY

A little boy sat at his desk at school. As he looked to the left, the little caramel-colored girl was drawing a picture of her mother, father, and two little sisters. As he looked to the right, the little vanilla-colored boy was drawing a picture of his grandmother, his mother, his little brother and his dog.

Straight across in front of him, the little crimson-colored girl was drawing a picture of her father, her brother and sister.

As the little boy sat there with his brown Crayola, and his manila sheet of drawing paper, his eyes began to fill up with water. To keep the other children from noticing, he laid his head down on the desk.

"Time to clean up," the teacher said to the class of first graders.

As the other children turned in their assignments to the teacher, the little boy with the tear-stained face stood at the back of the line. To each of the students, the teacher said, "Good job." As the little boy handed the teacher his blank sheet of paper, the teacher asked, "Why didn't you draw the picture of your family?" The little boy looked at his teacher, and with really sad eyes replied, "I don't have a family."

His teacher said, "Everybody has a family."

"Not me," said the little boy through his tears.

"Sure you do. Don't you have a mother? Don't you have a father?" the teacher asked.

"No ma'am. My mother died a few months ago, and I never knew my father."

"Oh," replied the young teacher, who was at a loss for words. "Well, who do you live with?"

"I live in a foster home with a bunch of other kids who don't have a family."

"Well," said the teacher, "then all of those other kids are your family and the grown-ups who take care of you are your family."

The little boy smiled. "I guess I've never thought about it that way," he said.

The next day the little boy handed the young teacher a folded piece of paper. As she unfolded it, a smile shone on her face. Her eyes met the little boy's eyes.

On the paper was a drawing of 10 children, in all shapes, sizes and colors. There were three adults in the picture as well.

All of the illustrated children wore smiles on their faces. The child with the biggest smile was the artist, for his teacher had taught him something very special. She taught him that he did indeed have a family.

THE SANTA LETTERS

At her desk, she sat. With pencil in hand, and paper tilted, she was ready. Ready to compose her letter. At the top of her paper, she wrote, "Dear Santa," in an illegible kind of print. With misspelled words and great enthusiasm, she continued, "I want a brown Barbie doll, a bike, a Cabbage Patch Kid, a Connect Four game, a Barbie Dream House, and a puppy. I've been good this year, except for that time I stole my brother's fifty cents from his dresser."

Seated across from her, a little caramel-colored boy had written his letter, asking Santa for a PlayStation 2, three PlayStation games, a motorcycle, a set of drums, some Spiderman action figures, and a little brother.

On the other side of the room, near the window, a little apricot-colored girl wrote her letter, asking Santa to help her daddy find a job. Then she added that if he had some toys left over, to please leave herself and her sister a doll. She added a P.S., and wrote that they could share one if Santa didn't have two of them in his bag.

At a desk in the corner, a mahogany-colored child sat alone. He had been isolated because he wouldn't stop talking, and he wouldn't sit down, or be still. His letter to Santa read, "I don't want my mommy and daddy to get a divorce. I want them to stop fighting and love each other, and love me too."

At another desk seated close to the classroom door, a pale-skinned little girl sat with a baseball cap on her head. In a very short letter, she wrote, "Dear Santa, make me a cancer survivor for Christmas. I want to live for a long time. That's all I want for Christmas."

Seated in the desk directly in front of the teacher's, a little peach-colored boy, with a dingy jacket sat. In really big letters, he wrote, "Dear Santa, I know you are not real because last year I asked you to make my daddy stop hitting me, and you didn't!"

At the end of the day, a fifty-seven-year old second grade teacher sat down with a cup of coffee so that she could relax. She picked up the stack of papers from the corner of her desk. It was an assignment she'd asked her students to do for as long as she could remember, *The Santa Letters*.

In the past she'd sent the letters home in a sealed envelope so that parents would know what their children wanted Santa to bring them. In the past, *The Santa Letters* had been amusing. However, as she read these letters, and her urge to laugh, turned into an uncontrollable urge to cry, she decided not to share these letters with anyone. Instead, she said a prayer for her students, and threw *The Santa Letters* away.

ARE YOU DEPENDABLE?

A little caramel-colored boy sat on the steps in front of his home. As he sat there, rolling his little red car across the porch, his mother stood in the doorway. Through the screen, she watched the small-framed warrior, who seemed to be waiting for something. She thought this because each time the little boy heard a car coming down the road, he would get up to see who it was.

"Son, what are you doing?" the mother asked.

"I'm waiting for Daddy."

"Oh. He's still at work. He won't be home for another two hours."

"Well," said the little boy. "I don't know how to tell time, but Daddy said that if I was good at school today, he would bring me a surprise when he got off of work. I was good today, so I'm waiting for him."

"Why don't you go play and when it's time for your Daddy to come home, I'll let you know."

Reluctantly, the little boy went into the garage and got his bicycle. As he rode down the street, he looked back to see if his dad was pulling into the driveway.

A few hours later, the little boy heard a familiar sound coming up the street. As he hopped on his bike and pedaled toward his house, he saw his father's beat-up old green pickup.

"Daddy," he said, picking himself up after falling off his bike. "I've been waiting for you."

"You were?" said the father, whose face was smudged and mirrored a tired look. "And why were you waiting on me son?"

"Because yesterday you said that if I was good at school today, you'd bring me a surprise when you came home from work."

"I did say that, didn't I?"

"Yes sir," the little boy replied.

"Well, were you good today?"

"Yes, Daddy, I was. My teacher said I was good. She put a star on my hand. See?"

The little boy proudly held his hand up so his father could see his shiny red star that had been stamped on the back of his right hand.

"Then, I guess this is yours." The father reached under the seat of his truck and pulled out a football. He handed it to his son.

"Thanks!" the little boy said with a big grin and really big eyes.

"Well son, when I can depend on you to do your part and act right at school, then you can depend on me to do my part."

With that thought in mind, are you a dependable person? Are you someone others can count on to keep your word?

Dependability is a character trait that our children are being taught at school. It should be taught at home as well.

The older generation had some words of wisdom that were supposed to help future role models. They were: "The only thing you have that you can give and still keep, is your word."

Be dependable because some child is patterning himself after you.

A MOTHER'S STORY

Tired and weary, she slowly walked to the bench. As she sat down on the cold, metal surface, clutching her purse, she tried not to think about how her feet and back ached, nor the calluses on her hands.

After a while, she looked at her watch. The bus seemed to be running late. A young man, about 20 or so, came to rest at the bench. Holding an umbrella in one hand, and wearing a back pack, he looked at the old lady with the crooked wig and worn coat, smiled and said, "Kind of wet today, isn't it?"

"Yeah, I reckon it is," she replied.

Noticing that she had no umbrella, the young man moved closer to her.

The old lady realized that the young man was sheltering her from the rain, and began to cry.

"Have you been waiting long?" he asked.

Brushing away a fallen tear, she answered, "Yeah, it's not usually this late. Are you a college student?

"Yes Ma'am."

"You make good grades, don't you?"

"Yes Ma'am," he answered.

"I had a son once. He was killed in a car accident many years ago."

"Sorry to hear that. Are you married?"

"I was once. My husband died in the accident with my son, and my daughter."

"That's sad."

"Well, nobody said life would be all happy times."

"Do you have any other family?" the young man asked.

"No, it's just me and my dog."

"Do you live around here?" he continued.

"No, I work down the street. How about you?" she asked.

"No, my friends do."

The young man looked at his watch. "You know, I didn't ask your name."

"Mae, Mae Johnson."

"Well, Ms. Johnson, I'm going to run back to my friend's house to find out what happened to the bus. And, I'm going to leave my umbrella with you."

"That's awfully nice of you, but you don't have to do that. I'll be just fine. A little rain never hurt nobody."

The young man ran down the street, and out of sight. Holding the umbrella in one hand, and clutching her purse in the other, the elderly woman closed her eyes and began humming to herself. Her song was interrupted by the honking of a car horn. She opened her eyes to find the young man stepping out of a blue car parked in front of the bus stop.

"Ms. Johnson, the bus isn't coming," he said. "My friend is going to drive us home."

The elderly woman, surprised, said, "That's really nice of you."

The young man helped the elderly woman from the bench to the car. Then he jumped in the back. "Okay Ms. Johnson, where do you live?" he asked.

"I live on Friendship Street. Do you know where that is?"

"Yes Ma'am, my grandmother lives on that same street, and that's where I was going."

When the car pulled in front of Ms. Johnson's home, the young man hopped out of the backseat and opened the door for her. Then he extended his umbrella, helped Ms. Johnson out of the car and up to the front door.

As she searched for her keys, she looked at the young man and said, "You are sweet. What is your name?"

"William."

"That was my husband's name. Anyway, I really appreciate all that you've done today."

"No problem," he replied and ran back to the car. His friend was about to drive off when the young man reached inside his backpack and pulled out a single red rose. "Hold up a minute," he told his friend.

William ran back up to the house and rang the doorbell. When Ms.

Johnson came to the door, he presented her with the rose and said, " Happy Mother's Day!"

Without giving Ms. Johnson a chance to reply, he ran back to the car.

When his friend asked him why he gave her the rose, he replied, "Because she was once somebody's mother."

THIEF ENTERS THE MIND

His Story:

My name is AL, and I have a story to tell. A few months ago I met a beautiful, caramel-colored woman. She was vibrant, smart and extremely independent. And because I like older women, this one was just right. Sixty-six years-old. The silver streaks in her hair didn't bother me, nor did her wrinkled hands, or pearly white dentures.

Gradually, I eased my way into her life. I began to tease her a little. I made her forget where she put important things. I'm so good at what I do, I even made her forget the names of her children. Because of me, she even forgot to pay her bills. After a while, I had her mind all mixed up.

I made her children worry; her daughter often cried. Her family blamed me for everything. But, I didn't care, because I had done exactly what I set out to do. I destroyed the mind of a perfectly healthy woman. I stole her wisdom. I destroyed her confidence, and replaced it with depression. I surrounded her with doubt and made her live in fear. Well, at least her family paid more attention to her.

I bet you think I'm horrible, don't you? The best part about me is that just like I stole everything from her, I have the power to do the same thing to you, and/or someone you know. And, there's nothing you can do to stop me!

Sometimes, that old lady who was once full of life and greeted everyone with a smile, cries to herself. She cries because she realizes that I've destroyed her life. She cries because deep down, she remembers how things used to be, before I came along and changed her world. She cries because even though she knows she's not crazy, everyone else thinks she is.

If I were you, I'd be careful. You never know who my next victim will be.

~ Signed, Al Zheimer

The Victim's story:

I don't remember my name today. I don't know why I'm in this place. This looks like my stuff, but it doesn't look like my house. My hair is a mess. I don't remember if I brushed my teeth today. I think I took a bath today. Maybe, it was yesterday. Hmmm, my dress is on backwards and my shoes aren't the same color.

There's a girl here with me. She says she's my niece. I don't even know her name. Maybe it's Lisa, no, maybe it's Sharon. Shoot, I can't remember.

I don't know why I can't remember. I think I'm supposed to go to work today. Oh, but it's 1 p.m. I think I was supposed to be there at 7:30 a.m. Oh well. I think I'll call my sister. Oh, what's the number? I think it's 7*5*-, umm, no, it's 4*9*, umm, 4*5*9, I don't know why I can't remember my brother's number.

I think somebody stole my money. I put it in my drawer yesterday. But, it's not there today. What is today, anyway?

I wish I had a good ice-cold glass of water. I sure am thirsty. I can't find where they put my cups. People always mess with my stuff. They think I don't know, but I know that girl who was here earlier took all my cups so I couldn't get any water.

Somebody's ringing something. Hello! Nobody's on the phone. Something's ringing again. It's the doorbell. The noise gets on my nerves.

I don't know that man standing there. He looks familiar. But I just don't remember. He looks like that man in the picture on top of the TV. I don't know why he's kissing me. He's a nice boy. Real polite. He's a nice boy. He called me Mama. I do have a son. Yeah, this is my boy. He looks like he needs to lose some weight.

He's saying I haven't paid my bills in two months. I paid my bills yesterday, I think. Maybe it was the day before yesterday. No, I think I said I was going to get around to it, *tomorrow*.

Why can't I remember? I can't seem to remember anything. This sure is an ugly dress I have on. I wonder who bought it?

I remember my name. It's, Mama.

The Facts:

Alzheimer's is a progressive disease of the brain that is characterized by impairment of memory and a disturbance in at least one other thinking function, such as language or perception of reality.

Early detection and diagnosis are essential to the well-being of an individual with Alzheimer's. The actual diagnostic work-up involves several stages: an initial evaluation, including a medical history, a clinical exam, lab tests and a mental status evaluation.

The Alzheimer's Association has developed a list of warning signs in regards to Alzheimer's, ranging from memory loss that affects job skills to changes in personality and loss of initiative.

Someone voiced the sentiment that beautiful young people are acts of nature; beautiful old people are works of art. Be attentive to their needs and changes in their behavior, and inform yourself about the thief among us.

TO WHOM IT MAY CONCERN

To whom it may concern;

You've seen me around. I am a teenager with no parental supervision. I am a teenager with no curfew and no rules.

I'm free to come and go as I please. No questions, no rules. No one tells me how to dress or how to act. No one corrects me when I'm wrong. No one cheers for me when I excel.

No one waits up for me when I come home late or says "I love you" for any old reason.

My parents are too busy living for themselves. There's no time for me. That's ok, because I've got a car and a cell phone. If I need money, my parents will give it to me. Just to get me our of their hair.

I make my own decisions, whether right, wrong or indifferent.

I could be doing drugs. My parents would never know. I could be getting drunk every night. My parents would never know.

I could be an unsafe driver. I could be a petty thief. I could be having unprotected sex. My parents would never know. You say I may have self-esteem issues? My parents would never   know.

I make ok grades in school. But since I have no parental supervision. I could probably get away with doing just enough to get by. My parents wouldn't know if I skipped classes. If I get caught, I can sign my parents' names just as well as they can. They'll never know.

My friends are envious. They wish they could be free of parental supervision - no one making them do chores, or questioning them about where they're going, who they're going with and when they'll be back.

It's great having no one telling you to do homework or insisting that

144

you change your outfit because you're revealing way too much. It's great having no one to tell you what kind of music is inappropriate, or which friends are bad influences.

Curfew? Getting grounded? Not in my world. Church and church activities? Not if I don't feel like it.

But sometimes, just sometimes, when I hear my friends' parents questioning them, I feel a little envious. I wish that I too had someone to care about me. I wish I didn't hate going home, to emptiness, to a house with no parental supervision.

I'll see you around.

OBSERVATIONS

*B*orn in a world where the color of one's skin matters more than the content of one's character.

*L*and where my fore-fathers died, and fore-mothers cried, because they were chained together and transported on ships to these, united states.

*A*merica, it has not always been land of the free, and the home of the brave.

*C*ourage, an important character trait that seemed to be born and bred in the African-American people.

*K*nowledge and wisdom shared by those who came before us serve as keys that unlock the door to our past that we call history, black history.

*H*oping that freedom would come, slaves relied on faith and prayer to see them through the pain, torment and suffering that accompanied slavery.

*I*nhumane was the treatment they received. Even worse than that is the way our young people are killing each other, the way drugs are ruining lives, and the way adults are abusing children.

*S*egregation, the separation or isolation of a race, class or ethnic group by enforced or voluntary residence in a restricted area, by barriers to social intercourse, by separate educational facilities, or by other discriminatory means.

*T*oday, we choose to segregate ourselves. For my parents, and grandparents, segregation wasn't an option, it was the law.

*O*vercome…we shall overcome, some day. When we learn to get along with one another, and stop hating one another. When we stop being envious of one another. Overcome, we shall, some day.

*R*espect for others and one's self is essential when trying to achieve greatness.

*Y*our ancestors had stories to share. Many were done in the form of coded songs. What kind of story will you be able to share that can be passed down from generation to generation?

*M*otivation? Every one must have it.

*O*pen your eyes and realize the part you play in society. Positive or negative, which one are you?

*A*chiever or underachiever, which one are you? Part of the problem, or part of the solution, which one are you?

*N*o one can hold you down, unless you let them.

*T*omorrow is a new day, with new opportunities to achieve greater things. It is a chance for change, and a time to contribute something positive to your community, to your culture, to your family, and your self.

*H*istory is symbolized by Marian Anderson, Benjamin Banneker, Mary McLeod Bethune, Cornelia Bowen, Gwendolyn Brooks, George Washington Carver, Shirley Chisolm, Fannie Coppin, Countee Cullen, Frederick Douglass, Althea Gibson, Prince Hall, Wallace William Jefferson, Mae Jemison, Barbara Jordan, Ernest Just, Dr. Martin Luther King, Jr., Mickey Leland, Willie Mayes, Thurgood Marshall, Doris Miller, Jesse Owens, Rosa Parks, Jackie Robinson, Wilma Randolph, Sojourner Truth, Madame C.J. Walker, Dale Wainwright, Venus and Serena Williams, Tiger Woods, Malcolm X and many others…and you, and me.

WHEN FOR WOMEN

WHEN little girls wish to be like their mommies, they want to wear heels like mommy and hats like mommy. They want to dress like mommy and put on make-up like mommy. They learn to walk like mommy and talk like mommy. They learn to sit properly like mommy and be courteous like mommy, because little girls want to grow up to be like mommy, to be a WOMAN. Let's hope mommy is someone to be proud of.

When dreams and goals must be set but somehow go unfulfilled; when you are taught that sticks and stones may break your bones, but names will not hurt you. They do!

When you know that prayer is the key and faith unlocks the door; however, evil is present on every hand. When you are laughing on the outside but crying on the inside.

When your last nerve has been agitated.

When your less than colorful attitude comes shining through.

When envy makes you green.

When that man you wanted so badly, the one you thought you'd just die for if he didn't notice you, turns out not to be the one for you.

When your heart gets broken, or maybe you must break a heart.

When those tears come rushing forward like a mighty windstorm and just when you think they've ceased, they've just begun to fall again.

When you hear people say that love will be better the second time around, and you think to yourself, "Is it really worth the energy?"

When you just need time by yourself, with no one else to interfere with your thoughts.

When you want to be beautiful for personal reasons, for self, for your own pride and dignity.

When giving up is not the answer and the solution to the problem seems inevitable.

When being loved by you, is important to you.

When those people who said you couldn't make it are forced to eat their words because you refused to let their negativity destroy you.

When winning isn't everything, but self-gratification counts.

When you can look in the mirror and your reflection smiles back at you.

When inner beauty is more important than outer beauty.

When your faith is weak and your courage has vanished, and your character has been destroyed, say to yourself, "Self, we'll be alright!"

And know beyond a shadow of a doubt, regardless of anything, or anyone else that you can make it, that you will make it because you are a WOMAN, a symbol of strength and encouragement and purity and intelligence and pride and beauty and trials and tribulations and charisma and spunk and devotion and ability and reality and companionship and joy and capability and respect and perseverance and effort and charm and versatility and honesty and curiosity and emotions and loyalty and opinions and vibrancy and opportunity and sensibility and tenacity and virtue and values and morality and motivation and independence and affection and dependability and determination and knowledge and fulfillment and intuition and sincerity and love and peace and wisdom and will power and perfection and education and hope and wealth and sensuality and personality and success and integrity and attitude and accomplishment and friendship and sisterhood and motherhood and womanhood.

You are a WOMAN! A symbol of greatness.

WHEN, FOR MEN

WHEN little boys wish to grow up to be like their daddies, they want to wear boots like daddy, and hats like daddy, they want to dress like daddy and shave like daddy, they learn to walk like daddy and talk like daddy, they learn to whistle like daddy and be proud like daddy; because little boys want to grow up to be like daddy, to be a MAN.

Let's hope daddy is someone to be proud of.

When dreams and goals have been set, but you just never got around to accomplishing them.

When you are taught that real men don't cry. They do!

When you know that faith cometh by hearing and hearing by the Word of God, however you don't really want to hear what God has to say.

When you are smiling on the outside, but dying on the inside.

When your kindness is (mis)taken for weakness.

When the expression on your face says it all.

When jealousy makes you hard to get along with.

When that woman you wanted so bad, the one you kept walking by so she could smell your new cologne, turns out not to be the one for you.

When your heart gets broken, or maybe you must break a heart.

When those tears you've been fighting break forth like a mighty thundershower. And just when you think they've ceased, they've just begun to fall again.

When you hear people say that if you just be patient, the right woman will come along, and you think to yourself, "Yeah, right. I'm not going through that again!" And so you build a wall around your heart so that no one can get close to it.

When you just want to be left alone, so that you can figure out what you need to do next.

When you want to look good for personal reasons, for self, for your own pride and dignity.

When giving up is not the answer but throwing in the towel is so easy to do.

When being loved by you is important to you.

When the person who said you'd never be anything, or that you'd never amount to anything is forced to eat their words because you refused to let their negativity bring you down.

When winning isn't everything, but it sure feels good.

When it's not whether you win or lose, but how you play the game.

When you can look in the mirror and your reflection smiles back at you.

When looking good on the inside (to God) means more than looking good on the outside.

When your faith is weak and your courage has vanished, and your character has been destroyed, say to yourself, "Self, we'll be alright." And know beyond a shadow of a doubt, regardless of anything, or anyone else, that you can make it, that you will make it, because you are a MAN! A symbol of stability and charisma and sincerity and strength and pride and blood and sweat and intelligence and dignity and ambition and curiosity and ability and confidence and trials and tribulations and honesty and opinions and leadership and capability and dependability and opportunity and reality and respect and perseverance and courage and sensibility and affection and motivation and values and morality and independence and versatility and joy and effort and charm and love and peace and wisdom and sensuality and devotion and will power and perfection and education and hope and wealth and personality and success and integrity and attitude and accomplishment and friendship and brotherhood and fatherhood and manhood.

You are a MAN! A symbol of greatness.

WHEN FOR CHILDREN

WHEN you don't want to listen to your parents.

When you don't think they know what they are talking about.

When you do things your parents have told you not to do simply because "everybody else was doing it," but, you're not everybody else's child.

When you say ugly things, and think your parents won't find out.

When you lie to your parents.

When you talk back to your parents.

When you are mean to your brother or sister.

When you are disrespectful to your elders.

When you do little mean things to hurt others.

When you misbehave in school.

When you cheat at school.

When you don't do your homework.

When you make bad grades.

When you talk back to your teacher.

When the teacher has to call your parents.

When your friends stop being your friends.

When you feel like nobody likes you.

When you feel like you can't do anything right.

When you don't feel like smiling.

When you question whether or not you are somebody special.

When you think your parents are being mean for no reason, because you didn't do anything wrong, and they don't understand what you have to go through, and they ground you even though it was somebody else's fault that you got in trouble.

Stop and think for a minute. Think real hard. Then, realize that you are somebody special because God made you. Remember that your parents love you and only want what is best for you. They were children themselves once before, so they do know what it's like to be "young". Remember that you are responsible for your own actions.

Follow the Golden Rule, which is "Do unto others as you would have them do unto you."

Remember to say "please" and "thank you" and "Yes Ma'am" and "No Sir."

Young ladies should strive to be sugar and spice, and everything nice, because "pretty is as pretty does.'

"Gentle" men are respectable, respectful, sincere and kind. If you present yourself in a positive manner, then others will have no choice but to judge you by the content of your character, rather than by the color of your skin.

Remember young people, life is what you make of it.

Respect yourself and others will respect you.

If you can't say anything nice, don't say anything at all.

Reflect on your life skills which are cooperation, patience, integrity, friendship, caring, effort, perseverance, organization, sense of humor, initiative, courage, common sense, problem solving, responsibility, curiosity and flexibility. These are the skills that you will need to carry you through life.

You are a special, unique and beautiful individual. Strive always for greatness, and remember when faced with a task or problem that seems impossible to conquer, that you can do all things through Christ, which strengthens you.

"LIFT EVERY VOICE"

While James Weldon Johnson was a school principal in his hometown of Jacksonville, Florida in 1900, he was asked to speak at an Abraham Lincoln birthday celebration. Instead of speaking, he decided to write a poem.

With time running short, plans changed again. Johnson asked his brother, music teacher J. Rosamound Johnson, to help him write a song. They titled it "Life Every Voice and Sing."

The brothers sent the song to their New York Publisher and thought little more about it. Once it was published and performed, the public found it hard to forget.

In 1920, Johnson became executive secretary of the NAACP. The organization adopted "Lift Every Voice and Sing" as its official song.

Many people who sing the song in February don't know all of the words or understand the meaning of the words. I did not have the opportunity to interview Johnson. A pity, because I would have asked him to elaborate on what each line means.

Still, I have my own understanding of each line had the song been composed today.

Lift every voice and sing.
(We need to be on one accord).
Till earth and heaven ring.
(And the world can be at peace).
Ring with the harmonies of Liberty;
(With equal opportunities for everyone).
Let our rejoicing rise
(Let us always project a positive attitude).

High as the listening skies,
(For everyone to see).
Let it resound loud as the rolling sea.
(Let the positive feeling affect everyone and continue to do so).
Sing a song full of the faith that the dark past has taught us,
(Tell others how you managed to make it through the hard times).
Sing a song full of the hope that the present has brought us.
(Tell others how blessed you are right now).
Facing the rising sun of our new day begun.
 (Each new day brings new possibilities).
Let us march on till victory is won
(Continue to strive for excellence, and great things will happen to you).
Stony the road we trod,
(The road might be a little rough right now).
Bitter the chastening rod,
(There've been restraints meant for unnecessary harm).
Felt in the days when hope unborn had died;
(At a time that made you feel like giving up).
Yet with a steady beat, have not our weary feet
(Even though you may be tired).
Come to the place for which our fathers sighed?
(You are not alone in feeling defeat).
We have come over a way that with tears have been watered,
(Someone before you toiled over a similar issue).
We have come, treading our path through the blood of the slaughtered,
(No excuse for a faint heart when others have sacrificed their lives for their beliefs).
Out from the gloomy past,
(Somehow you saw the light).
Till now we stand at last,
(Now you are rooted in pride and confidence).
Where the white gleam of our bright star is cast.
(You must continue to look up, and forward to greatness).
God of our weary years,
(When you were doubtful)
God of our silent tears,
(When you were distraught)
Thou who has brought us thus far on the way;

(A little voice inside encouraged you to persevere).
Thou who has by Thy might
(A force greater than you)
Led us into the light,
(Answered your prayers).
Keep us forever in the path, we pray.
(Let you not deviate from doing good).
Lest our feet stray from the places, our God, where we met Thee,
(Let you always be reminded of where you've come from).
Lest our hearts drunk with the wine of the world, we forget Thee;
(Don't let what the "world" says keep you from doing what you know is right).
Shadowed beneath Thy hand,
(There will be many opportunities for evil to loom about).
May we forever stand
(But you must choose to walk upright).
True to our God,
(Being honest and loyal to your Creator)
True to our native land.
(Being a productive member of the society in which you live).

THE KNEELING LADY

The kneeling lady sits alone
In a corner of the world
Where all is well within herself
Like a happy little girl.

The lady kneels for quiet sanctity
She kneels for inner peace
She kneels for self comfort
She kneels for spiritual release.

The kneeling lady thinks to herself
Of all that she could be-
Of hopes and dreams and glimmers of wishes
That let her soul dance free.

The lady kneels to say thank you
For all that God has done
She kneels in appreciation to
The one who gave his Son.

The lady kneels
This kneeling lady
Her body poised in grace.
Beauty is her character.
Colorless is her race.

Determination fills her heart
Perspective fills her mind
Courage keeps her going
Love makes her kind.

The lady kneels-
She is a symbol
Of loveliness in everyway.
As this kneeling lady
Takes the time to kneel and pray.

LAST THOUGHT

The only obstacles you cannot overcome
are the ones that do not exist...
you are bigger than any obstacle in your path.
Obstacles are like fog,
designed to temporarily block your view;
but never fear, the fog must evaporate...
and your clear vision shall be restored!
~cwf

ABOUT THE AUTHOR

CaSaundra W. Foreman has been writing since she was thirteen years old. Poetry was her first love. Her first article was published in a local newspaper when she was fourteen. She enjoys writing stories and poetry that will encourage and uplift others.

She is the author of *The Motherless Children* and *When An Angel Takes Flight/ The Light*. She has written for *The Afrikan Posta, The Waco Tribune Herald, The Brazos News* and *The Anchor News*. Her work has been published in the *Voices of Nature* and *Reflections Magazine*.

CaSaundra lives in Waco, TX, where she is Youth Director for the Doris Miller Family YMCA. She has two sons, Marquis and LaBraska, and a granddaughter, Mya.

ABOUT THE COVER

The cover was designed by Sherman Howard, III of Waco, TX. He is the owner of OnTheSpot Grapfx, and has been in business for over 15 years.

ABOUT THE BUTTERFLY

The butterfly is one of the most amazing, and unique creations on earth. Butterflies are blessed with two cycles of life.

They start out as caterpillars, then they go through a transformation, in which they become a beautiful butterfly. No two butterflies are exactly alike, just as no two people are exactly alike, and that makes them unique.

Just as butterflies go through a transformation, people also go through a transformation. They go through trials and tribulations, and either grow from them, or ball up into a symbol of depression, and fade away.

We all have the opportunity to transform into something unique and beautiful, just like a butterfly. Whenever you have one of those days when you feel like giving up, think about the butterfly, who starts out as a caterpillar, and then, goes into his cocoon, and waits patiently on God to transform him into something beautiful

Regardless of the trial or situation, be determined to come out of it beautifully, and transformed, mentally, physically, spiritually, positively and most importantly, triumphantly.

9 781456 732851